GOING AGAINST THE GRAIN

Faith. Life. Adventure.

NATHAN BLACKABY

CWR

© Nathan Blackaby 2018

Published 2018 by CWR, Waverley Abbey House, Waverley Lane, Farnham, Surrey GU9 8EP, UK. CWR is a Registered Charity – Number 294387 and a Limited Company registered in England – Registration Number 1990308.

The right of Nathan Blackaby to be identified as the author of this work has been asserted by him in accordance with the Copyright, Designs and Patents Act 1988.

For a list of National Distributors, visit www.cwr.org.uk/distributors

Scripture references are taken from the Holy Bible, New Living Translation, copyright ©1996, 2004, 2007, 2013, 2015 by Tyndale House Foundation. Used by permission of Tyndale House Publishers, Inc., Carol Stream, Illinois 60188. All rights reserved.

Concept development, editing, design and production by CWR.

THE SCREWTAPE LETTERS by CS Lewis © copyright CS Lewis Pte Ltd 1942. Used with permission.

Every effort has been made to ensure that this book contains the correct permissions and references, but if anything has been inadvertently overlooked the Publisher will be pleased to make the necessary arrangements at the first opportunity. Please contact the Publisher directly.

Cover image: AdobeStock

Printed in the UK by Page Bros

ISBN: 978-1-78259-058-3

Thanks to my friends and family for helping me find the time and words for this book.

Thanks to Jennie and the children for their support and patience.

To James, Alan, Jim, Everton, Carl and so many others who have spoken into my life in so many ways… thank you.

Contents

Introduction

Hi, and welcome to *Going Against the Grain*.

Before we get stuck into this, I want to start with just two questions: who am I, and who am I writing this for?

Who am I?

My name's Nathan. I've been married for 16 years, and have three children aged five, eight and ten.

I'm 38 years old, and have been a Christian for about 25 years.

I've studied graphic design, worked as a labourer, been a chaplain in a drug rehab facility for men, a church pastor and the CEO of an evangelistic movement.

Outside of my family, I enjoy time with mates, gaming, boxing, weights, motorbikes, art and YouTube.

OK – hopefully something on that list will relate to you. Essentially, I'm a simple Essex bloke and want to write a book about what it really means to me to be a Christian man. And that leads us on to my second question.

Who is this book for?

Maybe you connected with me in the fact that you are a Christian man, have been for a while and have seen and experienced a bit of what it means to follow Jesus. Or maybe you connected in other ways to who I am, but not the Christian man bit. Good – because this book is for you as well as the Christian blokes.

What I want to share in this book will hopefully challenge you Christian guys a bit about rediscovering the nature and purpose of your call to follow Jesus as your captain and brother; to dust off disappointment and disillusionment and reignite some of the fire that once filled your heart for Jesus and the Bible. But I'm also hoping that what I've written about will challenge you even if you don't believe in God or Jesus at all.

At CVM (Christian Vision for Men), we've often talked about how a majority of men in the UK think that the idea of God and church is some sort of crutch for the weak and vulnerable, not a 'real man' thing at all. Well, my hope is that by reading this you will see how, in actual fact, following Jesus as your brother, rescuer, captain and friend is the total reverse of that idea. I have found that following Jesus Christ and seeking to be like Him has taken me places I never dreamed possible. It has pushed me to the limits of who I am and shaken the dust from my life in the most exciting ways. Being a Christian man is, for me, totally life-changing – because this is more than just a set of rules to live by. This is about having a relationship with the living God. My life has been inspired by other men who call on the name of Jesus. I've seen the most amazing healing and restoration that I thought was impossible. Jesus has been a guide to me, a hope in the darkest of places and a continual friend.

Jesus has set me free as a man, and this adventure – this faith that has been awoken in me – is more than just me going to church on Sunday and chucking a few coins into the collection that passes by.

If you are genuinely looking for purpose in life – and are willing to take risks and develop faith in something that, as wild as it might seem is the thing that you know your life has been missing – then this is it. If you have sampled life's pleasures and still felt a desperate emptiness in your life, then there is a great truth out there for you. If you have been betrayed and hurt, cut by the people you love the most and feel (or have felt) like your life is literally held by a strand, then there is great hope for you. And even if none of that fits you, and you don't feel like there is a gap in your heart and life for Jesus to fill, then I want to encourage you to read on anyway – because one part of life that will come to us all is the end, and it is there that a hope in Jesus goes beyond this life and into the next. This is what we need to plan for, and ensure that the decisions we make now are the ones we want to impact that eternity.

I've worked with criminals who have murdered, stolen and destroyed. I have journeyed with people whose lives have been broken by affairs, financial disasters, disappointment and despair. I have walked with men who have wrestled with 20 years of drug addictions, where all of society's systems have failed them. But I have also seen families reunited, lives transformed, addictions broken, hope, love, truth and purpose restored.

This is what God does! This is what His Son, Jesus, is busy doing – and He calls us to be part of that action. Maybe you have looked into church at Christmas and thought, 'Nah, not for me, this has nothing to do with my life.' Or maybe you are a Christian bloke and you have felt lost and purposeless in your Sunday rituals. The good news is there is so much more… but not everyone will dig deeper.

I remember hearing a story of 100 soldiers training to be considered for the parachute regiment. They worked incredibly hard, focused on the goal. The reality, however, was that while they all stepped forward, only half of them would actually jump. The rest fell by the wayside – tired, distracted, disappointed, frustrated and looking to other things. For too long I had been that man – distracted, frustrated, disappointed with God or church or all of the above. It was from that place, however, that I decided to dig in; to not be embarrassed to say, 'I follow Jesus'; to not be ashamed to say I have faith in something bigger than what I can see, know and even convince anyone else of.

I don't know if you are still with me in this; maybe you have shut this book a few times and come back to it. So let's explore this stuff, be willing to ask questions, take a deeper look at the Bible and see if this really does have the truth in it that I am convinced it does.

The plan here is first to present to you some ideas and things I have seen in my time with CVM. Secondly, I want to explore the Bible with you and look at the lives of men who knew what this looked like. After each section in part one, there is an opportunity for you to read the Bible, and start to get used to exploring more than just a couple of verses here and there. If you have never read the Bible before, great! Get stuck in, ask questions, get confused and challenged – it is God's Word written down, and has the power to impact your life today.

Let's go against the grain.

Part 1

Finding the grains

1. Slight changes

Mike Massamino was part of a team of five astronauts tasked with a mission to service the Hubble space telescope in 2009. After two years of training, loads of practice, countless hours and days working on scenarios in the pool to simulate the conditions in space, they went for it. The Hubble was about 19 years old, and the spectrograph needed to be serviced – something that was never intended to be done in space.

When the team got out there and attached themselves to the Hubble, Mike went to work on the access panel. He had removed 117 highly engineered screws, each with success. Only a handrail was left to be removed, with just four screws remaining. Mike removed three of them, then – disaster. The bottom-right screw spun, and he stripped the screw head. Now, if this happens in your garage on a Sunday afternoon, it's a pretty big deal. What do you do? Who do you turn to for help? Now imagine you are in space – *space* – millions of dollars spent, hours of training for this single screw, the hopes of every telescope-gazer in the world pinned on you.

Houston, we have a problem.

The team in Houston calculated that 60lbs of brute force would break the handrail off and let Mike in (that's about 27kg for us). The trouble was that this action could spray debris everywhere – into highly sensitive space suits and equipment – and leave Mike with a razor-sharp piece of metal that could pierce his space suit, resulting in one or two further problems. Pressed up against Hubble, Mike found the strength he needed and *bang* – the handle was off and the multimillion dollar mission was back on.

I love that story. (If you get the time, watch it on YouTube – it's brilliant.) The reason I wanted to include it here is that going against the grain isn't always about massive shifts in your life, friendships and family. Sometimes even the smallest detail or adjustment can make incredible impacts in our lives. (OK, sometimes the changes needed are massive, but you get the point.)

Our lives are not always best defined as linear: they are more circular, and so often we can get lost in the transition between the expectation of what the Christian life will be like, and the reality of what happens when the wheels fall off and we are left picking up pieces. Circular lives revisit hurts and moments we have survived, but that's OK because this is the stuff that matters – as long as we keep moving forward and don't just stay stuck in this circle.

I learnt a new term recently and I think I can use it here: 'liminal spaces'. I think it fits. So often we can be in a place of liminality, that transition from one room to the next where we're not in either, but between, right in the doorway, right on the threshold. Apart from me trying to sound clever with my fancy terminology, I'm saying that being stuck in between is pointless, and if our circles in life keep us in a place where we can't move forward, then something needs to change – and fast.

Perhaps, then, it is in this working through and rebuilding that we learn some of the secrets of going against the grain. Getting splinters, cuts and scars and feeling alive is all part of the process.

As I write this introduction, I am sitting on a train. It's early in the morning, and I'm with a host of people who are either asleep, staring at their phones, or just fixatedly day-dreaming out of the window as the carriages quietly rattle along. It's so easy to fall into that indifferent attitude when it comes to being willing and ready to believe in God, or even having believed in God for some time but switched into cruise control. I want to feel like my decision to follow Jesus is like holding on to a lightning rod. It's real, scary, life changing, radical, dynamic, bold, brave, crazy at times – but never just drifting.

When Jesus called men to follow Him, it wasn't for us to drift through life, numb and continually searching for purpose, identity, value and our place in life. He equipped, prepared, sent out, empowered and tasked men to the frontline. The action and the battle were real. I think we need to go against the grain to find them again.

The Treasury

Welcome to the Treasury. In this section I'm going to suggest chapters in the Bible for you to read and reflect on. Each 'treasury' will provide you with a bit of space to write down anything you discover in your reading. I've tried to pick chapters in the Bible where the men and women went against the grain and found God in the process. Feel free to study these at your own pace.

YOU

Space to write something (or not).

2. Splinters

When I passed through puberty, I learnt an important lesson: when shaving, go *with* the grain of your facial hair. Shaving your neck, for example, upwards towards your chin (against the grain), clearly means you fear no pain and are happy to have a neck that looks like you shave your face and neck with 120-grit sandpaper. Point is, you go with the grain, not against it, when it comes to shaving.

If you want to plane a piece of wood hewn from a tree you've cut down, aiming to craft it into an awesome table, then going against the grain is probably not the option you would take. Not only is cutting down a tree or using a planer harder against the grain, when it comes to sanding and painting, the results will be poor.

Or imagine you're cooking for friends, and now is the time to impress with your secret culinary skills. You've gone for the steak au poivre, prepared with filet mignon. You look online and discover that your £30 steaks have a grain and need to be cut correctly with the muscle fibres, and not against them (unless you're like me, and it's the cheapest steak you can find, which goes off that very day).

There is a grain, a flow and a way in which things are done, and a set of expectations that attribute themselves to this pattern.

It's not just shaving, wood-working and butchery where going against the grain is widely ill-advised, as we see in various situations in society. Going against the grain is widely considered to be a deliberate decision to go against the socially accepted patterns or expectations of 'normal' behaviour, making your life difficult for no apparent reason. The idea of non-conformity, or to intentionally go against the grain instead of with it, is not a new idea at all – and I'm not saying we all need to be radical anarchists!

Let me try and explain a bit better. I remember sitting in church in my twenties, feeling fed up with all this 'God' stuff, thinking to myself, *I'm tired of hearing about what God is doing. I want to be part of it, not just a spectator. I want to see it. I want the action!* I gradually realised that I had been going *with* the grain in life, and even in my experience of church and what I thought a Christian bloke should be like, I was essentially just going along with it and never really challenging my own framework.

I think the trouble with this is that, for many of us, we've bought into the idea that all expressions of going against the grain in life are negative, and therefore ill-advised and actually a bit reckless – but are they? Or is it possible that, in certain arenas of our lives as men, there is something incredible to be unearthed, experiences to be had, stories and adventures to be chartered and battles won as Jesus puts us on the frontline? Perhaps I should throw in a disclaimer at this point: be aware that this course and decision is fraught with danger, trials, battles and maybe even scars.

I think that authentic faith in Jesus goes against the normal rules and expectations in our lives, and at times will be like sliding your hand against the grain of a lump of wood and getting riddled with splinters. But if you want to discover yourself, you need to lose yourself. If you go against the norms that have gently lulled you to sleep, you will get splinters.

I was fat and bored at church for years: fat on the pastor's sermons, and bored because I wasn't living anything out or applying it to my life. It was only when I went in a different direction with my time, passion, energy, money and faith that I started to feel like the sleeping lion in me, gorged and lethargic after 15 years of sermons and Bible studies, had awoken. That lion was getting agitated and poked and yes, it wasn't always comfortable, but stuff started to happen. My faith in Jesus became sharp, real, and restless. I wanted to see more and get involved; I felt that I had found some trouble and I liked it.

For years I had been inspired by the stories of other men who had seen God step in and rescue them, or of when God provided miraculously at the last minute; stories of countless lives turning to Jesus, and miracles; stories of unexplainable stuff being experienced. It always fascinated me. But then

I started to realise that these men didn't shy away from a few splinters – ones they received as a result of putting themselves against the flow and grain of life and holding on there, not just seeking stories and adventures to retell to the bloke down the pub, but pursuing Jesus and not letting their years fade by sitting on the sofa of what-ifs and if-onlys. These men carved out time for prayer, even when they couldn't see the answers, and this lifestyle of prayer cost them in time, energy and effort. These were men who gave money freely, not just from the leftovers but from the first lot they got their hands on. These were men who didn't just believe in forgiveness, grace, hope and trust, but who actually lived these things out when the fire was at its hottest. This is the call to go against the grain. It actually *hurts* to live that sort of Christianity, and you will get splinters and cuts all the time – but I know that our relationship with Jesus will be transformed. I know it. I don't want anything else.

The life of Jesus is the greatest message of freedom, joy and eternal life that this world will ever see. We can be friends with Jesus; we can be free men with a great purpose, identity and strength ahead.

But I also think that conformity – and the fear of getting splinters and really living out our faith against ridicule, failure and critics – has numbed and blunted the life out of loads of us. If that's you, then there is great news. Jesus calls men to go against the grain; to be willing to swim against the tide; to turn and face the wind, or, as a mate of mine called Mark once said, to run into the storms when they hit, not run for cover. Perhaps, like me, you've been formed and shaped to believe that going against the grain is a bad move, and instead it's better to conform, fit, stay put, not fight or fidget, just sit still and fear change.

Let's agree we're not having that anymore.

The Treasury: Noah

Genesis 6-10

It's so essential that we *mine* the Bible, and don't just cruise along with books like this one. The Bible, and only the Bible, is the Word of God written down, able to impact your life in the most remarkable ways.

As you read, consider Noah: a bloke who lived in a time of utter depravity, and heard from God to build a massive boat in the desert. He experienced ridicule, hopelessness and utter disbelief from those around him, but still he built the thing. Noah went against the grain, and refused to listen to the voice of his time. He had complete conviction that God was guiding him, and he was right.

YOU

Space to write something (or not).

3. Just a few words

I really want to encourage you to jump into the Bible, and not be put off by it or feel lost with it. There are loads of amazing ways to discover the Bible. I have spent a large amount of my Christian life just dipping in and out of it, looking for just a few uplifting words for my day-to-day, and it's simply not enough if you want to go against the grain and follow Jesus. In the past, I've bounced around various churches, sermons, speakers, Bible study apps and daily devotionals to try and feed that need for 'a few words for today from the Bible'. I was essentially looking for a power verse; just a verse for today and nothing more.

Yes   God can speak to you like this, and I am sure He does. Yes – there are loads of incredible resources out there to help us read the Bible. But I think there is more. In my searching, I found that most daily studies gave a Bible verse to read, but if it wasn't written there in front of me I wouldn't even open a Bible to read it – let alone bother to look at the 'further reading' section. I wanted the words for this moment, now and nothing more, but all I was reading was someone's reflection on a Bible verse I didn't even know.

When I dip in and out of the Bible with this attitude and even expectation, my faith life follows the same kind of hit-or-miss pattern. It's a bit like saying, 'Jesus makes me happy'. Well, that's OK if happy things are happening. But when your happiness fades and the world attacks you like a rabid dog and sets about making you pay, happiness quickly leaves you, and Jesus doesn't seem so close anymore. When we use the Bible to try to add a bit of niceness to our day, we are doing a similar thing. One day, you will hit a golden nugget and something will click – but then, in a moment, you will be like, 'Meh... didn't really interest me... wasn't where I'm at.' The point is, the Bible is more than this; God's Word is more than this. And as we explore it; mine it; shut our door and sit alone with it, God speaks deeper, greater and in ways that don't just make the day happy. They will transform your life.

I remember one unforgettable occasion when I learned a real lesson in this. I was visiting a prison in Brazil, a place built for 100 men but home to over a thousand. As I stepped inside to talk to the inmates about Jesus, my bottle went. I can remember frantically thumbing the pages of my massive leather-bound Bible for a quick word for today! A verse of courage, strength, boldness, direction or even escape would have done nicely. But nothing came to me in that moment. I opened the Bible, got lost somewhere in Proverbs, and gave up, greatly discouraged. I realised in that moment, when the heat was turned up, that in my head and heart

I had been surviving on just a few words, and not God's Word. I could have known and held in my heart the journey and moments of King David, and taken strength from his courage and boldness. Or the apostle Paul; his conviction and uncompromised charge forward to tell people about Jesus. I couldn't remember any of it, or find it in my Bible.

The important thing here is that I didn't beat myself up or choose to feel like an utterly woeful Christian. No, I could see the areas where I needed to apply myself a bit, so I have been doing so.

Let me land this with a practical tip and explore it another way. Years ago, I remember reading the suggestion that when you read the Bible, do it slowly, intentionally and pausing on each word – take... time... to... really... read... and... consider... the... words... you... are... reading. I found that this helped loads – not for large chunks, but maybe a short chapter. Reading it like this takes time, but it works. I can honestly say that taking a slow and intentional approach to reading the Bible has been so helpful to me.

I remember getting to know a guy who was in prison in Derby. He was the friend of a friend who had been imprisoned for life, and was talking a lot about how he had decided to follow Jesus after reading the Bible. This guy didn't have a church background, Christian mates, or any connection to Christianity at all. He just picked up a Bible and started to read it, mainly the Psalms (located in the middle-ish section). As he was reading the Psalms, he discovered a man called David – who was a king, but also orchestrated a nasty affair that resulted in the murder of the woman's husband. Reading about this in prison, this guy decided that, having read about David's life – full of mistakes and journeys back with hope and faith – he would follow Jesus. It was amazing to chat with him and hear about his life after accepting Jesus as his King.

The point of that story is to say that, even if you have never picked up a Bible (or the only time you did was to rip up the pages for Rizlas!), God can get your attention. We don't have to tackle vast reams at a time. This guy just started in the middle, and focused on a relatively short section – and that's all it took for God to get through to him.

The Treasury: Abraham

Genesis 12, 15, 16, 18, 20, 21 & 22

The life of Abraham (and his wife Sarah) is incredible. Years and years into their old age, God spoke and promised Abraham and Sarah a son – and then, after a few more decades(!) of waiting, they had that son who had been promised. Abraham had his 'wilderness moment'; he went with the grain on occasions (see chapters 16 and 20), he made a right mess of things, but then returned to God's way and God's timing. Abraham lived a life of going against the grain, refusing his own logic and reason. He learnt that real faith and trust in God might go against our usual expectations, but it is the best place to be.

YOU

Space to write something (or not).

4. The Einstellung effect

I want to try to deal with a few things that can really hold us fellas back from really going for God and being 'all in'. This stuff isn't void of my own personal experience; I have walked these roads, and it is from there that I want to write to you.

Some of us need to do some groundwork before we can fully let the handbrake off and go for this Jesus-life of overcoming our fears and doubts. If you can, read Luke chapter 15 in the Bible. This section includes the story of the prodigal son. Whether you have read it loads before or it is brand new to you, I'm going on to talk about it a bit – so it's worth having a look! (The book of Luke is in the New Testament, the second bit of the Bible, and is one of the four accounts of the life of Jesus from men who knew Him.) This story was being told by Jesus to help people understand who God is, and what He loves to do. Seriously – go and read it!

You might be wondering what I mean by the Einstellung effect. This is about a person's predisposition to try to solve a problem in one certain way (even if there is more than one approach), because they are impacted by their previous experience (often negative). So, basically, even though there is a better solution – a more appropriate attack or fix – our problem-solving is so guided by our past experience that the easier route just isn't seen.

This idea was tested by a few clever people in white coats, who set up identical chess boards in front of five chess masters. On the boards were two ways towards check-mate – one easier route, and one complex route. All five of the chess masters found the five-move check-mate but overlooked the much simpler three-move manoeuvre.

Here's the deal. In Luke 15, the prodigal son was on his way back to his father after making a total mess of his life, having blown all his inheritance and left broken by the choices he had made. As he was returning to his father, the son was working out the 'five-move'; the complicated way of earning his father's love once again by working as a hired hand, not as a son. But the father was having none of it. Guys, the father embraces that boy, puts a ring on his finger, a robe on his back and starts the party.

There was a simpler move back into the family, but the son's experience of guilt and shame made him feel that it just couldn't be that easy; that it had to be earned and not given freely. I think he would have initially struggled to accept the unconditional love offered by his father.

Maybe that's you; you're looking for a more complicated approach because you're fighting God's 'three-move', insisting that His love is earned, worked out and complicated. Well, it's not – so stop!

Surrender to God. Let Him put that ring on your finger and robe on your back. You're not here to earn anything; you haven't got to prove anything to God or do this or that to be right with Him. You just don't have to. It doesn't work that way. Just say yes to Jesus – maybe for the first time today, or for the hundredth time in your life. Stand again and let Jesus set the agenda, not you and your five-move strategy.

Some of this stuff can get a bit uncomfortable, but you need to know this: God delights over you.

Let me tell you a story from when I was working as a pastor in Essex. I popped out to the local Co-Op with one of my children, Micah, who was four at the time. Walking around the shop had been a little bit stressful, but nothing too bad. Then, for some reason that I will never understand, Micah didn't want to leave the shop at all. He had a major, warp-factor-ten meltdown. He lay in the store entrance screaming, legs and arms going in great erratic arcs as if he was trying to make a snow angel on the tiled floor. So I did the only thing a loving and caring father could do at a moment like this: I went and sat in the car and counted to 100.

Don't panic – the car was right outside the shop – but I just thought, *OK, you do that… I will be over here.* Micah, still making his frantic star shapes on the floor of the entrance, was now wedged in the automatic doors. They would shut just enough to squeeze him, then jerk open again as they sensed the obstruction. This didn't seem to pacify him either

– it just added a little rhythm to the meltdown.

When I'd made it to 100, I went back, lifted Micah up and carried my sweaty, flailing child to the car. Then I had a brainwave. I had done it before with him in a moment similar: I sang over him. I started to sing over my son as he wrestled in my arms. I told him I loved him, delighted in him. 'I love you, son, I delight in you. You're my son and I love you. I love you, son, I love you.' His wrestling eased and he breathed out a huge sigh of relief in my arms.

This one example from my life is just a fraction, slither and snip of the way God wants to delight and sing His love over you. I am willing to put a few quid on this, but I reckon that as you have just read that, you've done what my son did – you wrestled. 'You don't know my life; you don't know the mess; you don't know the pain, the mistakes, the shame, the hurt, the sin, the chaos. I am a geezer, and I don't like the idea of God singing love stuff over me. You can keep that, pal.' Well, you're right – I don't know any of your pain, fear, stress, shame, disappointment or anger, but I do know what it's like to go to God with all of that and feel Him delight over me. I can also admit that I am a little uncomfortable with the notion of God singing a love song over me too, instead I envisage my creator, King and master loving me for me, before I have even done or said anything.

Stop wrestling. Let God delight over you as His son. Let Him break the expectations of others and the expectations you yourself have carried. Go against the grain and let God work on the way you think about Him and yourself. You are a son – not a slave or stranger, outcast or unwanted. No effort you make will ever change this. You are a son of God. This makes all the difference.

The Treasury: Moses

Exodus 1-7
(You might want to keep going!)

Grab a cuppa and take some time to go over the life of Moses. If it takes a few sessions, do it – don't rush it. Invite the Holy Spirit to speak to you from Moses' life, and show you how his walk with God can impact your own.

The life of Moses is an encouraging story of how one man went from rags to riches to rags again, got loads of scars and wounds along the way, but emerged victorious because of his relationship with God.

Moses demonstrated an outburst of rage and personal justice that resulted in him killing a man, followed by a major identity crisis and a life on the run, involving him disappearing into the desert for a few decades. Moses went from the finest silks and foods – the perfumes and playboy lifestyle of the Egyptian palace – to sleeping in a field, spending long, hot days in the dry sun watching sheep. Moses didn't want to be a public speaker, was a very reluctant leader, and was worried and anxious about the path ahead – but he went against the grain. He chose to trust and obey, not from his own strength, but with a deep conviction that God was with him.

YOU

Journal a prayer, record what God might be saying – just write down something.

5. The frozen past

Clive Staples Lewis was the sort of man who managed to turn his hand to loads of academic things, and some of the things he said and wrote are just incredible. He held positions at both Oxford and Cambridge, and of particular interest to me has been his writing about theology (God talk).

I tend to have to read C.S. Lewis very slowly, because it's the sort of thing you can't rush (there are no pictures!). On one of my slow-reading days, I came across this quote, which I think is significant in this call to go against the grain:

'for the Past is frozen and no longer flows, and the Present is all lit up with eternal rays.'

Before I worked for CVM, I was pastoring a small church in Essex. It was a fantastic place, and as a family we loved being part of the church and getting to know some amazing people there. One day, I had a phone call from a lady who was part of the church community, but was in hospital dying from terminal cancer. Although I was in Sheffield at the time, I knew I needed to leave right then to drive down and visit her.

The journey went well, and I arrived before visiting hours ended that night. I had a little think in the car about things I could say, and what comforting words I would be able to bring to this wonderful lady in her final hours on this planet.

We talked about church and remembered some good times together, and then we decided to pray together before I set off for the journey back. I prayed the few things I had thought about on the journey down – nothing very interesting or significant; mostly about her future and the path ahead. I said a positive 'Amen' and ended the prayer well.

She opened her eyes, and in a soft voice she asked, 'Can I pray too?' Of course I agreed, and bowed my head. Let me tell you something: this dear lady had captured something unique that I was about to learn. You and I must live in the now because the past, as C.S. Lewis said, 'is frozen and no longer flows, and the Present is all lit up with eternal rays'.

What am I on about? Let me ask you a question. On your deathbed, if you are a praying man, what will your prayers be, if you get the chance to say them? I would probably mumble some insignificant ramblings about family. But this lady prayed not for the past, not for her mistakes, disappointments, or squandered hopes and dreams. She prayed not for the future, her safety, healing, or for fear to subside. She prayed for those in her heart – people living in the 'now' or the 'present' who didn't yet know Jesus as their Lord and King. As she prayed, I was moved to tears. I was just amazed at her priorities; the legacy she was leaving was incredible. She had realised that our best fight is in the now.

On my way home from the hospital, I did a bit of thinking. So often I am the type of bloke who lives in the 'frozen' past, trying to 'defrost' past moments, hurts, failures, and stuff that I did wrong (or the wrong that other people have done to me). All of these past events and moments are slowly defrosted so that I can re-experience that hurt – because, if I'm really honest, the hurt is real and comfortable at times, and easier to live with than without. It's an easy wall to sit behind and avoid the slow and painful work of having to dismantle it.

I've also found myself defrosting some of the good times with God, or 'God moments' when I had felt closer to Him – the time when I felt God speak to me through the Bible a few years back, or at church when I heard a good and relevant message for my life. Sounds OK, but the thing is, I was thawing out the good times with God because there weren't many new ones. I wasn't really praying much, reading the Bible, getting involved in church or wanting to hang out with Christian guys much; it was all a bit cold. Guys, this is not just a church or Christian man thing. We can end up doing this sort of thing in loads of different ways.

If I wasn't busy defrosting stuff from the past, I could be found wandering in my head way off into the future somewhere. Future hopes, plans or dreams, future fears or points of anxiety and concern were all mapped out.

Financial aspirations or dreams about earning more and saving more to buy more and then upgrade, redesign, build bigger and faster. Even our health and the questions that loom ahead can have us locked in a cycle of fearful daydreaming, while we worry about the great unknown around the corner.

Now here's the point to all this: I'm not suggesting that all our past reflection and future thoughts are negative. But whether you are stuck in the past or lost in the future, consumed with health, wealth or family what-ifs, you are being robbed of the 'now'. The 'now', says C.S. Lewis, is all lit up with eternal rays. The 'now' is where we operate, where we impact and influence change, and it is where we are forged as men with a ridiculous amount of potential, courage, hope, adventure and purpose. We need to channel all that into the frontlines where God is working, where Jesus calls us to stand – and that, men, is life-changing. (By 'frontline' I mean family, community, your work, your mates, your personal life and private life.)

I believe that C.S. Lewis was shouting at us that our enemy's (the devil's) plan is to keep us locked in the past or dreaming about the future, so that our brief stint on Earth will miss every possible moment and opportunity *now* to know Jesus more, and be like Him to our family, friends and everyone else we meet.

Let's go against the grain; let the past stay frozen so it no longer flows; let the future be shaped by God and trust that He's got it. Get busy living in the now and I think we will see some action.

The Treasury: Joshua

Deuteronomy 31, and Joshua 1, 5, 6, 23 & 24

I know this looks like a lot of the Bible to read, but let's keep drilling in and digging deep!

Joshua, and his role as Moses' successor, is a fascinating example of someone who trusted in God and went against the grain. Moses wasn't allowed to enter into the Promised Land – the mighty man of God who had led the people of Israel was shown his final place of rest still outside it. In response to this, Moses asked God to show him who the next man would be, and it was Joshua. Moses blessed him, and acknowledged God's new man for the mission. Amazing stuff – Moses just handed it all on, no founder's syndrome or sense of entitlement – this was God's glory.

Joshua did an amazing job too, and even more so when you consider the act he had to follow! Moses had been given the Ten Commandments, had seen seas parted and water pour from a rock. Moses was a man who knew the very presence of God, and had led for decades. Joshua could have completely crumbled in the face of this task, but he went against the grain and everyone's expectations. Joshua refused to be intimidated and overcome because he trusted God with outrageous courage and boldness. He led the people as a commander and conqueror of lands.

YOU

Space to write something (or not).

6. Safe and sanitised spaces

I was taken to church when I was young – youth clubs, meetings, the whole kit and caboodle – I could even say all the books of the Bible of by heart! I know, amazing right? On one occasion, my dad was speaking at church, and he got me up the front to do a live demonstration of my epic Bible knowledge. I remember walking to the front feeling confident – I had been sitting there practising – but as I got to the front, and faced the sea of people all looking at this young boy-genius about to wow them, my mind went *blank*. A panicked look at my dad told him the show was off. To this day, I can't remember all the books of the Bible. Perhaps I've developed a phobia – who knows, maybe that's why I get into a cold sweat when I look at the contents page of a Bible!

But having grown up going to church and being fully involved, church naturally became a safe, sanitised space for me. Things like after-church chat were all part of that clean, comfortable atmosphere. Maybe you've had a similar experience in a different setting. But I've often noticed that men who have drifted into that 'safe' space at church find themselves a bit lost. I'd describe these spaces like this:

The service has finished and you've been round a few regulars, saying something pleasant and nodding agreeably. You have a target: it's the tea and coffee zone, so it requires a few more nice 'hello's and 'hello mate, yeah, good mate, good's (it's Essex, remember!). You arrive at the tea and coffee; in you go.

Now you are armed with something to stand behind – a cup or mug of hot whatever – it's just something to break up the intensity of after-church chit-chat. The mug handle is far too small, but you stuff your fingers through regardless, while quickly demolishing a couple of stale custard creams to be washed down with a glug of tea. It's going well. Then comes the conversation.

There are probably a few men you default to for safe conversations. If they're not free, we could have a problem, but let's say they are.

'Hi mate, how's things?' the conversation begins.

'Yes mate, all good, been busy?'

'Yeah, you know how it is, keep going… How's the car?'

'Yeah, good, running well… You?'

'Yeah, great, holiday coming up, so, you know, little bit of time to chill.'

'Oh, nice one mate, yeah, I could do with that.'

'Right, well, see you next week, pal, later.'

OK, so you may be thinking, *That's not true, I don't get this at all – I love chatting to everyone and staying until the very end of church.* That's fine. This won't be true for us all, of course, but I believe it applies to a good number of us who go to church on a Sunday. For loads of the men we have encountered over years at CVM, this is what happens, and so many men on a Sunday play this routine, perhaps not even knowing how much deeper we could go with these friendships.

Let me pause for a second and ask you, then: what is the attraction for men to be involved in church? This might be a risky question to be asking, but if this is the type of conversation we have – after feeling a bit lost in all the singing because we can't physically make ourselves move to children's action songs and the talk was interesting but didn't inspire us – what's the pull? I ask because we need an answer.

If you're reading this as a bloke who isn't a Christian, you may be nodding with me here. I have loads of friends at my local pub who I play darts with every week, and each of them would say that the relationships they have, the stuff they are doing and the honesty and connection they have with each other is more real at darts on a Tuesday than it has ever been in their church experience.

I played the chit-chat game for years, generating conversations when in actual fact I would be thinking, *Mate, my kids are driving me mad, I am utterly exhausted with work, I am stressing about money, I've got this lump I've just found that the doc is worried about, my wife and I are struggling to see eye to eye these days…* It goes on. And in ten minutes of safe and sanitised Sunday conversation, not once did I ever connect with another bloke on the level I so desperately needed to.

This is why at CVM we advocate men's groups. Get men into the right environment and they will talk; they will do 'raw', they will do life, and yes – the guts will be exposed and the chaos and mess will be dragged to the light. The fantasies they can't tell their wives can be surrendered and dealt with; the affairs they have fabricated in a dream world can be banished in the safety of brotherhood and honesty. I have seen that this works, and I've been to many men's meetings where men have broken free from their emotional and spiritual prisons. Men in these environments are responding to Jesus for the first time. Do you need any more convincing? These are not men's clubs to trash-talk women and fertilise some sort of Christian misogyny; they are lifelines, hubs and splinter cells where men are broken and then rebuilt in stark honesty and friendship. This is going against the grain: not playing nice and topping up on Sunday niceness. It hurts, it is real and it develops courage and vulnerability – both of which are essential strengths that men need to build.

I've also realised that I tend to form safe and sanitised spaces in other areas of my life – not just at church. Left to my own devices, I choose to be alone; I don't generally reach out for new friends or look for the action. Even the darts nights I mentioned – despite really enjoying them, my wife still has to encourage me to go every Tuesday, otherwise I quickly get stuck in a rut of not going, or end up just watching the evening ebb away. Do I need to do another Myers–Briggs

Personality Type Indicator assessment? Maybe, but I think that for a lot of men, this is default behaviour that leaves a lot of us feeling alone, friendless and chewing on rubbish in life that could easily be dealt with and resolved. So what does this all look like for you? What are your safe and sanitised spaces that need 'messing up' so you can go against the grain?

The Treasury: Joseph

Genesis 37-42

Joseph is a fascinating bloke in the Bible – and he's one of the core chapters coming up in part two of this book, so I don't want to give too much away now. Have a read of some of the key moments in his life as some groundwork for when we look at Joseph again later. Take time with the Bible verses – dig deep and mine this stuff for yourself.

For now, let me tell you that Joseph went against the grain in a big way. When the fire was at its hottest, Joseph showed incredible self-control, discipline and resolve. Not only did Joseph stand firm in the face of temptation, he endured under the pain of isolation, abandonment and rejection, and he waited and waited. Going against the grain will hurt and it will cost you, but in the life of Joseph we can see it: the crown is there, and the prize awaits.

YOU

Space to write something (or not).

7. The art of celebration

Another way in which we can go against the grain is to revolutionise how we measure success. Putting it another way, we need to rethink how we motivate one another as men – in particular, in how we encourage and develop our lives as Christians.

I wasn't sure why, but I used to feel really discouraged about my faith, the effort I was making and how I felt my relationship with God was progressing. I think this was partly down to my interpretation of the messages from church, books and sermons, all seemingly saying that I needed to be a better man, and that who I am isn't the best I can be. I know that there can be a lot of truth in that sort of thing, but I think this has developed a culture that actually disarms men, and compounds feelings of disappointment and underachievement.

Let's think about messaging for a moment. Often, when men are addressed at church, it can sound like this: 'We need to be better men, better husbands, better fathers.' I'm not trying to suggest we don't need change – of course we do – but when the messaging to men is one-dimensional like this, it will slowly and gently erode our confidence and sense of worth and value; there isn't a measure or marker of success, so the bar will always be moving away from us. How will I know when I am a better friend; father; husband? Will someone notice that I have crossed the marker, hit the goal or achieved the target? What does this target, goal or marker even look like? If the messaging men hear is 'change, be better, change, be better', all we will reap is discontentment and a continual sense of failure.

How do we praise, value and recognise this stuff to motivate and encourage men to keep striving and pushing forward? We know that men respond to this stuff, and affirmation and praise are so important to inspire and infuse commitment – so how do we transpose this into a church format that inspires men? I started to see this in myself, and to be honest, this book has been written out of a pursuit to uncover and unearth this stuff. Why do men disappear into long hours of work patterns, sport and hobby commitments rather than church? Well, of course work is essential, and sport is fun and provides recreation, but there is more. These arenas are where men have clear and defined structures to affirm and praise – to value goals, targets and achievement – and this inspires men to connect.

So when I say that we need to go against the grain in this aspect, I'm talking about discovering the art of celebration as a way in which we can tap into this need to connect with men in ways they thrive from. I'm suggesting we build a culture of celebration that praises and cheers on: where men can acknowledge goals and milestones already achieved, but also a culture that celebrates even the slightest degrees of change.

If someone goes from being a fully-committed member of the League of Satan Worshippers (if it exists) and then surrenders their life to Jesus, we celebrate – big time! Their story is told far and wide; we make a great noise about it; the churches are packed, and rightly so! But if someone has stepped from –9 to –8 in their life, let's make some noise about that as well. If a vocally anti-God colleague of yours suddenly starts being friendly to you at work, that needs to be heard! That's going from –9 to 8. If you have felt overcome with doubt about Jesus, but then last week you encountered Him more closely, we need to share this stuff. It may seem small or silly, but I think it's the real and normal that will empower the army of men sitting on the sidelines, wondering what they can offer, still trying to decide if this 'God stuff' is for even them.

Deep down, I *know* that I can be a better husband, dad, friend, son, uncle, employee, employer and follower of Jesus – but if all I ever hear is the need for this change, I will quickly lose my enthusiasm for it. Let's celebrate the fathers, husbands, labourers, lawyers, the bus drivers, the Christian blokes, the not-a-Christian bloke who, after 20 years, has stopped smoking, swearing and drinking so much. Be the man who makes his voice heard; who encourages these men and sees their effort, their fight and resolve, their commitment and integrity. Call it out. Celebrate it.

This is not just a man thing – we need this functioning in the Church. I know plenty of women who need this encouragement, too. So let's go against the grain and be the men who instigate the culture shift.

The Treasury: Saul

1 Samuel 9, 10, 14, 15, 24, 28 & 31

Can you imagine being the most handsome man in England? (It's not easy, I can tell you…!)

Saul was the most handsome bloke in all of Israel, and stood head and shoulders (literally) above all the other men. He had serious pedigree – his father was loaded and influential. When Samuel saw Saul, the Lord spoke to Samuel: 'He will rule my people' (1 Samuel 9:17).

The reason I've included Saul here – the anointed king of Israel, triumphant in battle – is that he actually ended up going *with* the grain, not against it. Saul turned from trusting God and decided to go along with the pattern, expectations and advice of those around him. It went wrong, fast.

YOU

Space to write something (or not).

8. The labels we wear

As I travel around the UK with CVM, I see one theme that is consistent with men: we can default to defining our identity (and identifying other people) by the labels we wear. If you have ever been in an environment where you are meeting other men for the first time, or even subsequent meetings for a while, you will have seen these labels.

Let's start with the ones we don't even talk about: ethnicity, height, weight, the watch on your wrist, the car you arrived in, shoes, clothing, hair style (or lack of it), facial hair, tattoos, body language, walk, facial expression, mobile phone… the list goes on. All of this stuff forms the basis of our ideas about who this bloke is and whether or not we will get on. We also apply this to ourselves and, to varying degrees, we can live and act within this set of unspoken norms without realising it.

The next lot of labels are the ones that define us and can either be liberating or enslaving: failure, success, poor, rich, uneducated, healthy, unhealthy, lonely, ashamed, arrogant, prideful, anxious, fearful, bold, courageous, guilty, envious, loving, generous, greedy, kind, compassionate, hostile, peaceful, believing, disbelieving... Again, this list can go on and on – but you can see how easy it is to form our identity as Christian men around these values, and then project them onto others as we 'evaluate' them. We might know all this already, but I want to challenge us as Christian men to be able to hold on to what is good, and reject the rubbish that so quickly sticks to us.

I've seen small-talk move around a room the same way a hundred times:

'What do you do then?'

'I'm a builder.'

'Oh, OK, cool.' *Level established; ranking system engaged; I know where I fit and what the expectation is here.*

I'm not suggesting that, when asked about what you do, you reply: 'Oh, I'm an internationally acclaimed brain surgeon, just having a break from surgery – between things, you know, off to Dubai tomorrow.' (Unless that's true, of course.) No, to go against the grain with these labels is to not let this stuff define who we are *and who we think others are*.

It can be all too easy to sit under the cosh of labels and their ability to reduce our courage, faith and boldness. We'll explore this some more in part two, but I want to do the groundwork now. Failure, shame and disappointment seem to me to be the top three labels that us fellas most commonly find stuck to our lives (anger is another big one). I have seen them numb, disempower and imprison some of the most awesome men of God I've met. To live effectively as Christian men who go against the grain, we need to learn how to reject this way of thinking. This is not to pretend that the rubbish that has formed these labels never happened, or that the sense of failure we feel isn't real or the disappointment doesn't still hurt. It's about refusing to let these labels define who we are. As we refuse to feel unworthy because we don't earn a lot, or because we never achieved a decent education, or whatever our labels are, we start to feel freedom. And the most liberating thing about this is, once we start to live without these labels in our own lives, we stop attributing them to others so often. Instead, we take labels from the Bible and from who God says we are – and who our neighbours are.

The call to live as Christian men is a continual process of refusing the labels the world would have us wear, and accepting the ones the Bible holds. Easy to do? No, not at all – but this is one of the reasons I love being a Christian. It is hard work, and it requires dedication, commitment and at times even a 'broken spirit'. I want to suggest that all this can be discovered in the crucible of relationship, where guys have the close friendships with other men that allow the real and raw questions and emotions to surface. When we step into these unique environments where men care about each other; hold one another accountable; allow each other to speak into the situation and stand with undefended hearts – stuff happens. It can take time to lower our veneers of expectation and projected self-image, but as men start to 'do' honesty in a small group of brothers, we *will* see a radical shift in our lives.

The Treasury: David

2 Samuel 5, 8, 11 & 12

After Saul came David, the shepherd-warrior. David was the youngest (and smallest) in his family. He was the absolute last person anyone expected to be king, yet he became a king of great influence, power and victory. David learnt to lead, fight and command, but even after all his campaigns and adventures, in his last hours he was alone with a family in ruins – so, not the perfect life, but one that was lived against the grain.

David had shown mercy when he could have dished out justice; he'd shown courage in the face of adversity, and he picked himself up, even when God disciplined him. That's going against the grain.

YOU

Space to write something (or not).

9. Conform or be transformed

Last year, Carl Beech (CVM's president) wrote a book called *The Way*. It talks about the process of not responding and acting how the world might be expecting, and instead pursuing a different way of living. Beechy (as Carl is affectionately known) based his book on what the Bible calls the Beatitudes (a section of Jesus' teaching about how we should live), and it's well worth a read, but here I want to briefly touch on this counter-cultural way of living that Jesus suggests, and how it works.

Christian men will still encounter multiple situations that push us to the limit; to the edge of where our faith impacts how we act and react. Take road rage, for example. It's a thing, and might be an arena where your faith is called out. Do you explode and chase the bloke who has just cut you up? Do you slam on the brakes as the person behind you sits on your bumper? I remember driving early one morning with my wife, when I accidentally cut up another driver. I could see her angrily pulling alongside me, so I turned down the audio Bible I was listening to (that's the truth!) and wound down my window. She was coiled like a snake, ready to pour out scorn and curses at me, when I waded in with, 'I am so sorry, didn't see you there at all, please accept my apology.' She looked as shocked as my wife was! This was, if I'm honest, a million miles from how I have been known to act in such moments. The lady drove away, and my wife sat there in amazement (it doesn't always go that well). So that's just an example – what about your reactions in areas like this? When you have been wronged and hurt, for instance, or spoken badly of and feel the cut of injustice at your name being tarnished, do you retaliate on social media by throwing mud back until you feel better? Do you choose to love and show generosity even to those who don't deserve it – and especially to those who have hurt you? Can you reach out and help or encourage someone who never does it for anyone else? Can you bless someone when your natural reaction is to curse them?

This is such a dynamic and radical code for Christian men to live by, but what a remarkable thing it is. The world doesn't work that way – it just doesn't – so to say that being a Christian is to act and operate like this is no small ask. In fact, it is a supreme undertaking for the committed and focused, who are determined not to shrink back from doing this stuff, and to love others even when it really hurts.

We have the choice to either conform to the pattern of the world around us and act as everyone expects us to, or choose a different path ('The Way'). The different path is found in submission to God, allowing the Holy Spirit to transform our minds and hearts. (Yeah, you can find this in the Bible – have a look at Romans 12 and read the whole chapter to get the context.) I believe it's through this counter-cultural lifestyle, and a habit of turning our lives against the expected patterns of this world, that Christian men will discover identity, purpose and fire in our lives. We forgive when everyone expects revenge; we bless when people call for a curse; we give when people look for us to take back; we stand with the person everyone else has walked away from; we choose to love when all we see is hate.

History has been punctuated with examples of this in the lives of people like Nelson Mandela, who refused to hate after the injustice of his incarceration. Then there's Mother Teresa, who turned her life and hands to the care of outcast children whom others despised and rejected. But just imagine for a moment men all over the country – men who have a real and authentic faith in Jesus – acting with this spirit. Men who live beyond what their own strength can achieve or resolve to do; men who literally turn the world upside down with their refusal to act as the world expects; men who show forgiveness, grace, love, compassion, generosity, kindness, gentleness – when the world calls for the opposite. Now *that* would be amazing. And if you still think that being a Christian is for the weak, the wimps and the brainwashed, I hope you are beginning to see this as the greatest battle you'll ever be in!

The Treasury: King Asa

2 Chronicles 14-16

Let me throw you a curve-ball in the shape of King Asa. You might have read about him before, or maybe this one is brand new to you, but take some time to read these verses and, as always, invite the Holy Spirit to inspire you.

Asa came face-to-face with over a million fighting men who wanted him dead. He could have done any number of things, but he went straight to God: 'Help me!' Asa looked for God and instructed the people to do the same, and they found victory. Amazing stuff! But later on in his life, Asa lost sight of the going-against-the-grain thing, and decided to go *with* it instead: easier, quicker, makes sense... right? Not exactly. Have a look.

<u>YOU</u>

Space to write something (or not).

10. Breaking for the best

I started my role at CVM with a couple of mugs. No, not anyone you would know – actual mugs. (Sorry, but it made me laugh!) I had two mugs that I used to illustrate a talk: one that I had broken and glued back together, and another that was good as new – not a scratch. My talk would be about how our lives can be a bit like a mug – then, when stuff happens (health scares, money issues, whatever), life gets real and the mug starts to break. Your marriage, your career, your faith, your family can all take a hit, and soon you find yourself in pieces.

Carrying on with my mug metaphor, I also had a lamp switched on (with no lampshade – just the bulb). I would put the whole mug on the lamp, so that no light was getting through. After smashing the other mug (and often cutting myself accidentally in the process), I would reveal the mug that was glued back together – in a mess, but still holding together. I would then put the broken mug over the lamp, and the light would burst through all the gaps. The point was that God's glory shone so much more through the broken mug than the whole one. Simple, and I'm sure it's been done loads before, but it spoke to me so deeply.

Giving in to God's timing and wisdom, and letting the mug (us) yield under the weight and chaos that life can hurl at us to then be put back together by God is, without a doubt, painful. I think that many of us fellas get close, but then turn back. Surrendering to God is brutal at times and can take us way beyond the forced Christian smile or mask on our face on a Sunday morning or in the company of others (is it just me doing those?). There is something incredibly unique and precious that can be won from this process of breaking, but the process is called 'breaking' for a reason. We hold on, wrestle and twist; we fight and wriggle and pull and push; we squirm and dodge and sidestep before we yield. I have fought to the very limits of my own strength before reaching the point where I yielded, not always because I wanted to, but because I had no strength left to fight with. Yet it has been in this (eventual) yielding to the Holy Spirit that I have seen the most dramatic breakthroughs in my life. Forgiveness, gentleness, peace, kindness, joy, patience, self-control, goodness and love have grown in me, showing more of my relationship with God than ever before.

Do I still wrestle with this? Yeah. Do I still feel lost in the scale and scope of who God is and how miniscule I am? Absolutely – all the time. Am I utterly dumfounded by the work of the cross and why Jesus would die for a guy like me? Yes. Do I still have doubts and questions? Yep. But I have known the presence of God in the breaking; I *have* known Him through the times in my life when stuff has been painful. Maybe you're with me on this one – the breaking and the yielding to the Holy Spirit. What I mean is *surrender*. Surrendering to God in your life is more than just words – it will take you to the limit, open you up and bare all. The apostle Paul wrote: 'It is no longer I who live, but Christ lives in me' (Galatians 2:20). I think this is it: I think this is the place of surrender that not only says yes to God, but is a life that knows what the reality of that decision is all about. At CVM we talk about a high calling for men to follow Jesus, not just a Sunday thing (there's no such thing as a passive walk with the God of the universe). This is a call to *come and die, come and die*.

Maybe, like me, you have felt a sort of tension within, a force or pull in one direction when you want to go another way. Perhaps, even now in wanting to know more about God, the wall goes up. You want to believe and trust, but there is a call to walk away. The Bible talks about this when Paul says: 'I don't really understand myself, for I want to do what is right, but I don't do it. Instead, I do what I hate ' (Romans 7:15). A tension – a war and a conflict – is going on because this breaking work is not always done through disasters in our lives; it can be felt and experienced in the little things too. Think about it. The secret opportunities to grow lust in your heart and dream of the maybes with the attractive people on your radar. The opportunity to cheat on a form or add a few pounds to the expenses. The banter that turns nasty towards one bloke at work and you're invited to jump in and add fuel to the fire. Checking the emails late at night knowing that a hive of porn is just a click away. The tension and the choices are all there.

But these are the moments in our lives where we get a radical opportunity to go against the grain: to pull over and let that bloke who is driving on your bumper go past. To turn off the laptop and just go to bed. To stand up for the guy at work who is being systematically bullied. This is the stuff that needs to break, as it is needed to shape us and the journey Christian men take. This is the breaking of the vessel; this is about surrender and yielding to a King who doesn't operate in the way the world does. Lives lived like this will impact others in the most incredible ways.

The Treasury: Daniel

Daniel 1

I thought it would be interesting to look at the way in which Daniel refused to go with the grain. He had somehow found himself in a prestigious job. Influence, education, power and position – he had it all. All he needed to do was eat all the food from the king's table and stay fit and strong (and remember that going against the king was a really bad life choice). But Daniel refused, while others went along with it.

He flatly said no. I don't want to spoil this – maybe you know the story already – but go and have a read, because going against the grain will have amazing results when God is involved in the decision.

YOU

Space to write something (or not).

11. The truth, the whole truth

I think one of the devil's best weapons against us men is to keep us in a cave, holding on to the rubbish of our past and shaping fears about tomorrow. It's all lies. He *lies*. I hope you read that last bit – let me say it again: the devil lies.

Perhaps the concept of there being a devil is a weird one, and you don't agree. That's fine. However, even though we may want to, we cannot gloss over the fact that the Bible says that Satan exists. As the enemy of God, Satan seeks to steal, kill and destroy (John 10:10) – something we certainly can't deny goes on.

The lies the devil puts together are like onions: these bad boys are layered, and no matter how you cut them, it's going to sting. The lies are bespoke, hand-crafted, tailored to fit our individual situations. You can be in a meeting or driving your car, when *bam*, a lie made just for you is delivered, no signature required. Fellas, I have experienced this many a time, and it is often at the start of something positive. If I take a stand for my faith – if I feel like God is doing stuff, or I try to commit to praying or reading the Bible more – the co-ordinates are locked in, and lies are inbound. If I try to orchestrate prayer times with my wife, the lies are locked and loaded and on their way.

In the past, I've found myself consumed with these lies for ages. As they did laps in my head I felt exhausted, fed up and depressed. My prayers stopped, and reading the Bible felt toxic – but when I finally brought it to the surface, I realised I was dealing with 100% lies! The damage it had done to me for so long was ridiculous, but the lies had felt so true.

The Bible sometimes describes the devil as the 'father of lies', and his intention is to destroy, distract, divert, undermine, question, doubt and undo what God is working on in our lives. This is like a blindness that keeps men from seeing the truth for what it is, and also from really living all-in when it comes to following Jesus.

So, how do we see the lies, call them out, overcome this stuff and then return to sender? Our going against the grain of lies is layered too, because some lies might even feel comfortable, masking who we really are: 'You don't need to change these areas in your life – everyone else does this stuff. You're not the only bloke to look at porn, so don't be so tough on yourself.' 'You've been hurt before by this person – you don't have to forgive them. They will only hurt you again, so it's actually better for you to not forgive this time. Look after yourself.' Lies can attack our value, worth, character and abilities. But they can also feed our greed, arrogance, false humility, and the way we interact with and treat others too. Layers – loads of them.

The lies that swirl around my head seem to always be linked to either the past or the future. (Remember what we said about the frozen past and the complex future?) Lies about the past are often focused around failure, shame, guilt, or the stuff that sounds like, '*You*!? Why would you do that? You don't know enough, you've never been able to this or that...' Blah, blah, blah. Lies that attack our future focus on fear, anxiety, failure, potential problems and stuff that we worry might happen. Again, this might seem obvious – but when it's tailored just for you, it will find the chink in your armour. The point is, see it: spot the lie quickly and drag it into the light (truth). Don't pull it in and give it a home.

Sometimes along my journey as a Christian man, there are times of wilderness – months where prayer seems to hit the ceiling and fall back down, and reading the Bible is like wading through treacle. It all seems to be much harder work, and even going to church and feeling like I fit there can be an uphill slog. These seasons are not especially new or a revelation to anyone, but I have found that lies exist in these places of wilderness too. Jesus experienced this in His own life and I think we can. Stuff like: 'God's not with you anymore, He gave up on men like you years ago.' In the desert places we might experience on the Christian journey, the lies will be a partner on the path, and they need to be dealt with.

Bringing lies into the light can be done on our own,

but sometimes we'll need to be more strategic with it. In dealing with lies in my own life, I've found it helpful to be active in the following ways:

First of all, be alert! Know how to identify the lies, and call them out – quickly.

Then, consider the *truth*. Ask, 'What does the Bible say about this, or me, or the situation?'

Get the Holy Spirit involved in the fight. Invite Him to help you discern the lie. Then drag it to the surface in the company of others. This has often released me from lies about myself; the perspective of others can help deal with this stuff more decisively.

Reject the lie, and be ready to keep rejecting it; refuse to let it stick. Sometimes this will be a minute by minute, on your knees, calling-out-to-God battle; other times, it will be years later when you're in supermarket aisle six and considering baked beans with reduced salt when *bam* – it's back, full strength. Reject it again.

This isn't easy – this really is going against the grain. To bring lies out into the open and decide not to hang on to them takes incredible courage, resolve and discipline. To surrender this stuff – even the lies that make us feel important or valuable – makes us vulnerable in front of others. Go against the lies that say men don't show emotion, and the lies that keep men from turning to help in some attempt to save face, or protect their pride. To fly in the face of this stuff is empowering, and the call on Christian men to be like this is unique. It hurts; it will push us to the limit and stretch the core of who we are, but it is there that we find greater freedom, purpose and identity.

The Treasury: Daniel and his mates Shadrach, Meschach and Abednego

Daniel 2-3

So, what do you do when the king decides that prayer is illegal, and anyone who doesn't pop outside at prayer time and bow to man-made statue shall be killed in the most horrible way? Would you have a prayer time in a place where you can be seen, caught and killed instead of bowing to the statue? No, not sure that would have been my first choice either.

But for Daniel, it was. He refused to go along with the rest of society, bowing to the false god, because he believed in only one God – and he wasn't about to stop praying to Him. Cue the lions, the screaming and the horrible death…? It's time to explore how Daniel was a man who refused the norm and seriously went against the grain, whatever the cost.

YOU

Space to write something (or not).

12. Learning to think big again

Have you ever been around people who just love to think big? It can be such an unsettling feeling but it can also be amazing. A good friend of mine, Alan (big Scottish bloke), is totally wired for thinking big. When we meet up, he starts with a minute of chit-chat, then *bang*: 'Nathan, have you considered this...?' I usually need time to get to grips with the scale and scope of Alan's ideas, which are usually on a scale a thousand times the size of the one I'm working on. I think this is something people in business learn to do really well, like another guy I know called James. With a business background, big deals, big conversations and jobs getting sorted, conversation with James is always big; big faith, big God, *big*.

I want to tell you a story – well, two, actually.

First, let me take you to a dry and dusty day under the Latin American sun. You are near Copiapo in Chile, at a mine called San Jose. The date is 6 August 2010 (you might remember this story). Thirty-three miners have been trapped underground after a slab of rock the size of the Empire State Building broke away, trapping them all 2,000 feet below. After six hours, the dust cloud seeps away and the men, the scene now clearing, are able to get a better look at their home for the next 69 days. Up on the surface, teams are being assembled, and one account describes how there is only a 2% chance that these men can possibly survive.

Let me fast-forward over this story and share one particular detail. It was reported that, while the men were trapped underground, the local leader decided that a large white cross should be installed to remember the lives of those 'lost'. He called up a sculptor friend of his (I don't know his name, so let's call him Colin). Colin built the cross, which, in reality, was a tombstone being built over the lives of living men.

You can read online about how the 33 all made it out alive, went on a world tour and ended up almost worse than before (it's a story full of twists and turns, that's for sure!). But it's the tombstone over their heads that bothers me the most.

At the time of the Chilean mine collapse, I was also in Latin America, which brings me on to the second story I want to tell you. I was working for Teen Challenge, a drug rehabilitation project in Recife, North East Brazil. We received a phone call from a lady asking us to help her son, Rodrigo, so we drove out to their home to see them.

As we walked into the room, the air was hot and close, and the humidity was so intense that I immediately felt water on my skin. We walked into a darkened bedroom, where slices of sunlight sprayed into the room at different angles, lighting up a young lad in his twenties, sitting on a thin stained mattress with his head on his knees. Drug equipment was all around him. Most of the light was coming from a hole in the wall, where a chain had been brought through and was fixed around the young man's ankle. His mum, in a desperate attempt to stop her son from escaping and getting another drug high, had literally chained him up, knowing that if he escaped, he would meet certain death at the end of the local dealer's revolver.

I remember standing and looking at Rodrigo, broken and ravaged by his drug addiction. I paused and tried to take in the situation, then looked at my friend and said, 'Irmão, vamos, eu acho que nos não podemos ajuda esse cara.' ('Brother, let's go, I don't think we can help this guy.') The truth is, I wasn't able to think big. I looked and my mind and heart told me that this guy's life was over, and no amount of help would save him. I effectively started to build a tombstone over the life of a living man. Thankfully, my mate, Everton, refused to do the same. He invited him home, and over the next year he hugely and sacrificially invested in his life. Rodrigo made a full recovery, discovered he could play the guitar and sing, and gave his life fully to following Jesus. I watched from the sideline the whole time.

This experience, and others like it, made me realise that we need to learn to dream and think big again when it comes to what God can and will do. We approach God based on what we think is possible, rather than what we think is *impossible*. When we approach God with the impossible, then really we just start to open the door to what actually is possible. Does that make sense? Most of my prayers are based on the possible, and not forged from a sense of impossibility. I want to rediscover the art of dreaming so big that it is ludicrous to imagine it happening.

Our generation desperately needs men who have a faith that is not without blemish and scar, but one that is real, raw and has been broken open; a faith that is willing to ask, think and dream from a place of impossibility, rather than possibility. I think Jesus calls men to be this type of follower. When that translates into how we live out and share our faith, can you imagine the potential? The ideas? The boldness and the noise we could make? Now that raises the bar, just a bit!

The Treasury: Esther

Esther - read the whole book, go on!

OK, I want to set you a challenge here: read the entire book of Esther. It's ten chapters, and will probably only take you around ten minutes a chapter (some are very short). All in, it won't take much longer than an hour – job done. The story of Esther is amazing, because she was not only used by God in the most incredible way, but she overcame crippling fear in the face of extreme danger.

Esther really went against the grain of self-doubt, fear, anxiety, the what-ifs, the why-mes and the *I could actually die doing this* moments. She found herself on the frontline of a potential genocide, and she was placed by God strategically for that moment – but what would Esther do? Run, hide and stick her head in the sand, or push against her fears and doubts?

YOU

Space to write something (or not).

13. Hello, Trouble...

Gerber Gear (a company that makes outdoor kit) recently did an advert simply called, 'Hello, Trouble'. The advert is clever, it's gritty and raw, and somehow it connects with me. Whenever I watch it I get that fizzing on my skin – that feeling of, 'Yeah, I want some of that action!'

I have often found myself drawn to the men around me who are unafraid of risk, and the stories that tell of the trouble-seekers, the space monkeys and the pioneers. It's like standing in front of the TV as a child, watching the slightly overweight moustached fella in the red leotard and bike helmet slide down the barrel of the circus cannon. With a blast he is launched high into the air, grasping a moment of flight – having been willing to risk being blown to pieces. (I was a child, so it impressed me!)

Do you know what I mean? More recently, I was reading and watching TV documentaries about the SAS and their foundations and early life under the leadership of David Sterling. These men were the renegades; they pushed and questioned; they were not happy to conform and play nice, they wanted more than that. Most of them only in their early twenties, these young men were pioneers on the edge of discovery and innovation, which is where this stuff always seems to happen. Only when they were jumping out of moving trucks to see the best techniques to survive, or hurtling towards the ground testing the limits of the parachute did they innovate, create and break through.

I am not suggesting you go to these extremes, though I have to admit that some of the stuff these guys do is desperately appealing to me! You see, these men discovered that in just groups of five, they could cause absolute carnage behind the enemy lines of the Second World War, but their impact completely depended on the bloke next to them getting his job done. If one team of five failed to take out a command post or fighter squadron miles up the road, it would leave the other outfit utterly exposed. They had a comradery and dependence on one another that was held on a knife-edge, but it was real and it worked. It was on that knife-edge of win or lose – guts and glory – that they pioneered and found the most remarkable creativity.

OK, here is the point. I feel like going against the grain is to push and press, to fight and wrestle for this pioneer spirit again. This will mean taking on the title of this chapter and welcoming trouble along your path, and to invite the chaos is no small matter. I have seen men take a stand and decide to go full throttle, no handbrake, no safety net – and they have been utterly smashed up. They have been through some of the toughest storms imaginable, but they have held the line – the knife-edge where chaos meets innovation, where disappointment and despair collide, where fears are forged into courage – and this is the place I actually want to be in.

It's so easy for us to buy in to the normality of life. The ruts are deep and once our wheels sink in, we can be there for a long time. The ruts rob us of creativity, passion and the pioneer spirit. It's a bit like saving up and buying a caravan – a chance to travel the world, to dream and think big. You hook up the van and away you go, the location and road uncharted. Soon, you find a great spot, and decide to keep going to the same holiday park   it's nice, good food and facilities, an easy option. After a while you look at your caravan and decide to lift it up on some blocks, as it's been a while since you have moved it. The wheels come off (no real need for them at the moment anyway), so you store them in the garden to be cleaned up for next summer's travels. But that summer never comes, and instead you look at your now static caravan, and decide to put up some trellis and a small fence to claim your part of the site (others have, and it looks nice). A set of steps go in, proper floors, windows, and a drainage and electricity hook-up. Step back from your caravan – originally intended to be your pioneering vehicle – and what you have created instead is a static, going-nowhere box with an ornamental garden and a deckchair in which to sleep away your afternoons.

This is what can happen spiritually and we must rage against it – we *must*. Maybe you're in that place now, or maybe you're not even a Christian but can see how this could happen. I don't think this was ever the call to follow Jesus; to set up a static faith in Him.

So many of the men in the Bible we've looked at kept on pioneering, believing, moving forward – not always complying and looking perfect, but it was real. Faith is most dynamic on the edges of chaos in a pioneer heart. As your life and faith in Jesus (at whatever stage) connects with the desire to dream, think big and look for trouble. I think it is here that we find something unique.

As we develop our generosity, our courage, hope, trust, forgiveness, love, mercy, grace, compassion, kindness, peace – all of these things, when really lived out and fused to the pioneer will be dynamic, compelling and transformational. This is what it looks like to refuse to take the wheels off the caravan, and invite God to take you on journeys, on trials and up mountains that will test you, shape you and refine your life.

The Treasury: Philip

Acts 8:26-40

Philip was a man who was looking for trouble. He wasn't running and hiding; he wasn't searching for a rut to sit in for the rest of his life; he was the opportunistic man. He was a pioneer like so many of the disciples he had journeyed with. He was out there – fierce persecution had scattered the Church, but Philip was on the edge of chaos, taking the opportunities, looking for the knife-edge moment where trouble meets opportunity. I love it.

YOU

Space to write something (or not).

14. Hear the Spirit

Let's end part one with something I think we need to be really aware of: the voice of the Holy Spirit.

If you are reading this and exploring what it means to be a Christian man, the Holy Spirit is an essential ingredient. Essentially, the Holy Spirit is God, just like Jesus is God (there being three different functions and elements of His character, but all equally God). I know, this is one of those mysteries I just don't fully get – but neither does anyone else, so you're in good company.

Nevertheless, in showing you a glimpse of what it looks like to be a Christian man, this is a fundamental person to speak about. The Holy Spirit is the ingredient that will bring the change, bring the power and the ability for us to go against the grain; it is His work which lets us even identify the grains in the first place.

In the Bible, the Holy Spirit has moved in some amazing ways – with great power and force, but also like a whisper. So often I find myself waiting for the biggest and most eye-catching action from the Holy Spirit: the gift of tongues (speaking in a language that isn't your own), being knocked over by the power of the Holy Spirit and getting my white fillings turned into gold. (If that happened, I would pull them out and sell them – maybe that's why it's not happening…)

Here's the deal: I think the Holy Spirit gently broods over us at times, and prompts us not with a bang or a fanfare, but a whisper. (We will see this more when we look at Elijah in part two.) As men who have decided to follow Jesus, the Holy Spirit is part of the relationship – and it is essential we listen for His voice.

For example, my wife Jennie recently went to McDonalds with one of our children, and while she was there, she felt the Holy Spirit prompt her to tip the young girl at the till. A bit weird, really, but Jennie lives her life looking for these whispers and prompts. She took the 'happy meal' and gave the girl an extra pound coin as a tip. The girl was amazed – a bit confused, but more amazed – and Jennie could see the boost in her self-esteem. The manager looked on and smiled at the offer, and it seemed to boost the self-esteem of the other cashiers too. I like that – it was simple. A person was seen and encouraged, and I think the Holy Spirit does this sort of thing all the time. Was it this girl's first ever shift? Was she feeling anxious? Maybe – but it doesn't really matter. So often we won't know what the impact is, but we respond anyway.

On another occasion, I was driving to Harlow (where I was living at the time) and noticed a sign saying, 'Psychic Fair this Sunday'. I felt a nudge from the Holy Spirit, almost a sense of indignation, so I resolved to go that Sunday and pray against what was going on. I sat inside the building in Bush Fair, praying that God would be glorified; that the impact of this stuff wouldn't work, and that Jesus would be present. I did that for a few hours, then went home and thought nothing more of it. A couple of years later, I got a phone call from my mum, telling me that her cousin (a pastor) had finally managed to set up a church in Bush Fair – in the building the Psychic Fair used to use! They'd also been praying for the opportunity for years. I liked that – it was just a small prompt that had got me out of my seat and doing something. On that occasion, the impact was a good one and I actually found out about it.

Here's the point, fellas: the Holy Spirit wants to have control in your life – He doesn't want to be suppressed and controlled, muted and ignored. I believe there will be plenty of opportunities for you to respond with your time, voice, wallet and energy. But will you see them?

Going against the grain here is the process of intentionally saying yes to this stuff, even when it feels and looks slightly odd. It's being willing to give, share, help, encourage, invest and equip others as the Holy Spirit guides you. You may get it wrong, you might look stupid (at times you *will* look stupid), but go for it! Tune your ear to His voice; notice Him doing small and intricate stuff in and around your life. And just a closing remark: if you are not seeing this stuff and you want to, then ask. It really is that simple.

The Treasury: Nathan (the prophet)

2 Samuel 12

I absolutely love this story – it has one of those 'Oh, you mean me, then' moments when the penny well and truly drops. Nathan is given the lovely task of going and telling a king he's a rotten sinner and has been found out. Nathan, like so many prophets of the Old Testament, faced kings and rulers, great armies and enemies with absolute confidence that the message God had given them would be spot on.

YOU

Space to write something (or not).

Part 2

The men against the grain

Welcome to Part 2 – we made it!

If you've been a Christian a while, some of the stories and names here might be ones you know already. Perhaps you consider yourself to not be a Christian but are still reading – cool. I want to encourage you to stay with this, look up the Bible sections, and take some time to explore. Please don't just take what I write here; the purpose of this is to help get us into the Bible, because that is where the work is done.

OK, let's drill down and explore how these men had a faith that went against the grain, and how God shaped their faith and life.

Jacob

Read Jacob's full story in Genesis chapters 27–33.

First, let's set the scene for Jacob. His name meant 'deceiver',
'supplanter', or 'to trip up' or 'to overthrow' – and his life
started much like his name, really. He was born holding on
to his twin brother Esau's ankle (after they had 'wrestled' in
their mother's womb), and later he put together a massive ruse
(with his mum's help) to steal firstborn Esau's birthright. (In
Israelite families, the firstborn son was given the birthright
status from the father, often on dear old Dad's deathbed.)

To cut a long story short, Esau was rather upset when he realised what had happened, and started to plot and scheme ways to murder Jacob. After that, the brothers went their separate ways and the relationship was pretty much destroyed.

But the key thing to note here is that, even though Jacob cheated his brother, their father, Isaac, gives Jacob a blessing and God responds to it. Isaac prays this over Jacob:

'May God Almighty bless you and give you many children. And may your descendants multiply and become many nations! May God pass on to you and your descendants the blessings he promised to Abraham. May you own this land where you are now living as a foreigner, for God gave this land to Abraham.' (Genesis 28:3–4)

And God honoured that – Jacob went on to have 12 sons (and a daughter), who became the 12 tribes of Israel! That's a *huge* family, and they went on to 'supplant' and overthrow many nations and people in (and around) the land God had promised Abraham. Interesting, that!

Living up to his name, Jacob knew how to deceive – his mother, Rebekah, had taught him the art of how to dress like someone else, sound like someone else, and even feel(!) like someone else in order to trick Esau out of his birthright. So you might have thought that Jacob, fraudulent mastermind, would see a ruse coming when he stayed with his uncle Laban. Or not…

Laban had two daughters, but it was Rachel who had caught Jacob's eye (the Bible tells us she had a great figure and face – good to get the details). Rachel's sister, Leah, had a twinkle in her eye and a bit of life, but it was Rachel that Jacob loved. Cutting another long story short (but I'm summarising what you've already read!), Uncle Laban got Jacob to work seven years for Rachel's hand in marriage. But somehow, by the end of the wedding, Jacob discovered he had married her sister Leah instead (easy mistake to make). Understandably confused (and probably somewhat upset), Jacob argued the case, did a deal and decided to work another seven years to get the wife he always wanted: Rachel.

So Jacob ended up with two sisters as wives – and as you might expect, a certain animosity grew between them when Leah could conceive, but Rachel struggled to have children. Both sisters gave Jacob their servant girls to have children with (in a 'How many kids have you had with him, then?' kind of battle), and on and on it went.

Jacob's family had grown, and he was moving across great areas of the desert. After leaving Uncle Laban, God moved Jacob and settled him again. Rumour had it that Esau wasn't far away, so Jacob sent messengers of peace to his twin brother to try to smooth things over. Jacob had reached out and made the first move, but word came back that Esau was already on his way with 400 fighting men! But despite the fear and sense of impending chaos, Jacob chose not to run, like he had done so many years previously, and decided to stay and face this head-on (we're starting to go against the grain now). Remember, Jacob was the 'deceiver' – he knew how to manipulate and trick others, and had experienced this himself.

The Bible tells us that when Jacob heard his brother was on his way, he was terrified. Talk about skeletons in the cupboard just waiting to jump at you! Stuff in our past can lie dormant for years. We know it's there – like something in the boot of your car that moves around occasionally – but normally it's ignored. So Jacob slept on the issue and then thought he'd try to appease his brother by sending him a load of gifts – 'stuff'. You can imagine the moment for Jacob: *Maybe gifts will soften him... maybe I can buy my way out of this one.*

In the middle of all this, I want to pull to the surface the fact that, though Jacob had made a mess of things in the past, this was a defining moment for him. He could have run; assembled an army; laid traps; hired private security; argued his case at the local courts. But he didn't. In Genesis 32:9–10, we read the incredibly humble and broken prayer offered by Jacob. No running for him – no scheming and plotting this time. Jacob had made the first move for reconciliation, sent gifts to prepare the way, surrendered it all in prayer and then braced himself for whatever was coming over that hill. And their reunion would be remarkable – a real tear-jerker (check it out for yourself).

But what came over that hill first of all was a man of God

(or God Himself!) who wrestled with Jacob until dawn. Bet he didn't expect that! Jacob refused to stop fighting the 'man', and would only let go if He blessed him. Well, a bizarre night and a dislocated hip later, Jacob is renamed 'Israel' by God. Amazing.

For Jacob, going against the grain was about determination, resolve, refusing labels and seeking reconciliation. Jacob refused to always be known as the deceiver. He refused the label and the mistakes of his past – he wanted blessing, and to draw a line in the sand. Jacob showed remarkable resolve to keep working for Uncle Laban for 14 years, having been ripped off and cheated, but still he persevered. He also showed willingness to seek reconciliation by being the first to move forward with his brother. These acts of Jacob are defining enough, but I think the clincher is in the fact that, while wrestling with God, it would have been easy for Jacob to say, 'I've messed up; I stole this; I deceived this person; I failed, and got it so wrong.' But instead he presses on, accepts his new name, with all of its incredible meaning and the promise that God doesn't forget His word. Jacob doesn't sulk or wallow in self-pity. He goes against the grain, and is up and moving again, worshipping God (only now with a limp).

Sometimes the journey as Christian men requires us to yield to God, to surrender control and give over the reins; at other times, the surrender will look a bit different. For Jacob, I think that 'surrender' was more about letting go of everything but God – he didn't want the land he had, the cattle, the wealth of the life he had collected. He held on to God in the hope for something new, a new name and a blessing. He refused to let go. When we submit to God and let Him have full control, we essentially hang on to God even more.

Joseph

'But the LORD was with Joseph in the
prison and showed him his faithful
love. And the LORD made Joseph
a favorite with the prison warden.
Before long, the warden put Joseph in
charge of all the other prisoners and
over everything that happened in the
prison.' (Genesis 39:21-22)

Read Joseph's full story in Genesis chapters 37–50.

Has life ever been rough for you in that, without justification,
your name has been slandered or your reputation shredded?
Have you ever found yourself in the middle of a nightmare
situation despite having acted to the best of your knowledge
and ability? I think this is one of the things that hurts the
most, especially when your name and character are slated,
bullet-ridden and attacked – even more so when it comes
from people you know or love. I have personally been on
the end of this stuff, and I know how quickly it can happen
and how much it can hurt, and how it can leave you lost in

frantic reflection and self-doubt.

Joseph's life is an incredible example of how a person can be cheated, mistreated, lied about and wrongfully represented – and still be an amazing, godly bloke. His story might be one that you already know, whether you're a Christian or not. Jason Donovan played the lead in the theatre version of *Joseph and the Amazing Technicolor Dreamcoat* (classic!). That version of the story obviously focuses quite a lot on a posh coat – one that Jacob gave to his favourite son, Joseph. The Genesis version of events is well worth checking out in full, but, rather than retelling the whole story, I want to fast-forward a bit here to look at how Joseph really went against the grain.

Joseph had dreams – and while he didn't explicitly say, 'Hey, brothers, you were all bowing to down to me,' that's what his dreams were showing. Quite obviously, Joseph's brothers didn't share his enthusiasm. They hated him, and plotted. They pushed him in a pit, ripped up his coat, covered it in blood, and while spinning the lie to their aging father that he'd been eaten by a wild animal, they had sold him to slave traders. His *brothers* did that.

As a slave, Joseph ended up in Egypt, but being strong, smart and reasonably attractive, he landed himself a good job with a decent boss – a rich and influential man called Potiphar. Now we get to the part where Joseph's integrity was challenged. Mrs Potiphar (we don't know her name in the Bible) was not exactly shy in her advances towards

Joseph, but he was having none of it – good man. He got away from the situation, but she held on to his tunic. Long story short, she tells her husband that Joseph had tried to assault her. Needless to say, the boss is less than thrilled, and has Joseph thrown in prison.

Joseph sat in prison for at least two years, so let's take a quick summary here. He was betrayed by his own brothers, who faked his death and sold him into slavery. He worked as a slave for more than a decade without complaint. He did the best he possibly could, rejected the advances of a wealthy married woman (the boss's wife, no less), only to then be accused of sexual assault. He was thrown into prison and forgotten about for years.

What would you have done in that situation? Would you spend each day protesting your innocence, demanding your right to a phone call? Would you hatch a plan of escape? Would you daydream about returning to take revenge on your brothers and Potiphar's household? Have you been wronged like this? Have you been lied about, cheated, robbed, or had various other injustices set against you? Hurts, right?

I'm pretty sure it hurt Joseph too, yet what we have here is the most remarkable going-against-the-grain imaginable. He didn't fight or plot revenge where he could have fought to clear his name and contest his innocence. Instead, he trusted and hoped; he waited and held on to God being sovereign, even fighting the feelings of rejection, loneliness and fear.

You will need to read the story in full to see what happened, but it's amazing – and Joseph does get to see his brothers again. Big stuff happens.

Joseph refused to behave how the world expected him to. He chose another way, another path that went against the grain. I find his example astounding because choosing to go this way when we are hurt and cheated – instead of taking the path of hatred and revenge – takes more strength than is humanly possible. It requires divine intervention. Joseph was a man who knew God, and that was the game-changer in his life.

Gideon

"'But Lord," Gideon replied, "how can I rescue Israel? My clan is the weakest in the whole tribe of Manasseh, and I am the least in my entire family!" The LORD said to him, "I will be with you. And you will destroy the Midianites as if you were fighting against one man."'
(Judges 6:15-16)

Read Gideon's full story in Judges chapters 6–8.

OK, let's get the backstory for this one first. We pick up this story with the Israelites not living how God had commanded them, so God had allowed them to be treated harshly by a rougher group of neighbours (the Midianites). The Bible tells us that this bunch treated them so badly that the Israelites ran into the caves and started to dwell there, fearing for their lives. I love the way the Bible includes this stuff, as we get the background. It says the enemy hordes were as 'thick as locusts' (Judges 6:5). Can you imagine that lot taking your animals, crops and food, and pushing you up into the mountains? Not a good situation at all.

It's worth mentioning here that this was a common pattern for the nation of Israel in the Old Testament. God rescued them from Egypt, where they had been slaves for hundreds of years, and agreed with them to be their God (and they would be His people). Well, time and time again they changed their minds and did their own thing, so God let them get on with it. Each time they would be pummelled by an enemy, starve, wander around lost, and then cry out to God for help again. Each time God restored them, and this occasion would be no different.

This is where we find Gideon: the next contender who went against the grain (literally!). Gideon was threshing wheat at the bottom of a wine press (not where you would normally do this job) – probably hiding grain (and maybe himself) from the Midianite oppressors. While Gideon was there, an angel of God appeared to him. (We're not told what the angel looked like, but Gideon had a good chat with him, so let's assume he was human-looking.) The angel said this: 'Go with the strength you have, and rescue Israel from the Midianites. I am sending you!' (Judges 6:14).

My response would probably have been this: 'Er... have you seen this lot? They are a horde of locusts – brutal killers who have rampaged and ravaged our whole community. And, sorry, did you say the strength *I* have?!' Gideon's response isn't a million miles from that: 'how can I rescue Israel? My clan is the weakest in the whole tribe... and I am the least in my entire family!'

The Bible goes on to tell us that Gideon prepared some food, and the angel of God consumed it with fire. Then Gideon went on to tear down the altars and poles that had been set up in the community to worship false gods (it sounds nuts, but read it!). After that, Gideon needed just a couple more moments of reassurance to make sure that God really was with him in the epic punch-up that was about to go down.

Let's just pause for a minute. When I talk about going against the grain, I want to show you that, as a Christian man, this stuff doesn't always make sense. Gideon is a prime example of this: he was the weakest in his family, his clan was the smallest, he was in hiding, terrified for his life, and God called *him* to be the man leading the charge. Why not a giant, a warrior, a battle-proven commando with a string of purple hearts and a CV of combat accolades? Because God calls us to think big – way bigger than you and I are comfortable with. He called Gideon to think so big that there was absolutely no way the battle could be won unless God turned up and did the business.

I believe that Christian men are called by Jesus to think this big – to allow themselves the willingness and courage to think about the impossible as possible with God. I have worked with loads of men who had been written off by the world, only to see God do the impossible with their lives. They've been restored, rebuilt, and gone on to smash the biggest obstacles in their lives. Men who had lost all trust in their relationships and been cut off from family and grandchildren because of drink and drug abuse: I've watched these same men return with clean lives to these families and seek forgiveness, reconciliation and restoration after meeting with Jesus. I don't believe there is anything else that can transform the life of man like this – only Jesus Christ.

God challenged Gideon to think big and to trust Him with everything he had. But there was still more in store. Gideon raised his army, only for God to tell him he had too many men. Sorry, what now? Essentially, what God is saying is, 'Tell the lads that if any are afraid, they can go home again.' So 22,000 men walked off (there were only 33,000 in the first place!). Then, as if that hadn't rained on Gideon's parade enough, God tested the fellas again, eventually leaving Gideon with just 300 men. From 33,000 to 300. Ouch.

This is all I can say, men: as Christians, we are called to go against the grain; against our head and our heart at times; against our logic and reason at times; and then, when we have done that, God might take us even further than we believed possible. Is that easy? Does that sound like the easiest option to you? No, it doesn't to me either. Imagine Gideon marching towards the Midianite army with 300 of his mates. If victory was going to happen, it would only be because God showed up – but guess what, He did! Read about it in Judges 7. It really is amazing stuff.

You will face situations in your life where trusting in God will seem like absolute lunacy. The world will scream at you that you are mad and, like Gideon, all you will hear is disbelief. But trust in God. Trust in His Word, His promises and His love for you. Will it always work out? Will we always win how we wanted to? Maybe not, but that doesn't mean we don't need to trust. The trust we are offering goes beyond getting the result we wanted; it is a trust that says, 'Even if this doesn't work out so great for me, I am trusting in You, God.' You see, the rubber hits the road in the rubbish in life: the cancer treatment, the prayers for a dying child, the agony and the hurt and the confusion. We stand in that place and we trust, even if we don't see the outcome we want. Does that sound like the easy option? No, and it isn't. But it's going against the grain.

Elijah

"'I have made no trouble for Israel," Elijah replied. "You and your family are the troublemakers, for you have refused to obey the commands of the LORD and have worshiped the images of Baal instead. Now summon all Israel to join me at Mount Carmel, along with the 450 prophets of Baal and the 400 prophets of Asherah who are supported by Jezebel."' (1 Kings 18:18-19)

Read more about this part of Elijah's story in 1 Kings chapters 17–19.

Another aspect of going against the grain is the process of overcoming the crippling disappointment and despair that can be the undoing of so many men. We can be cruising along, when *bam* – a lie, a conflict, a failure or a disaster can tip us into despair or have us running for the hills (or, in this case, a cave). I believe that the call on Christian men is to know where these caves of despair and disappointment are, but be willing and ready to come out of them again, stronger and with a lot more fight in us. I want to show you that achieving this is linked to something called a 'revelation'.

If you ever thought that the Bible was boring or lacking action and adventure, take a look at the life of Elijah. This is a man who battled, was fed by ravens, and ran in front of chariots. The part of the Bible I want to explore with you is a section called 'The Contest on Mount Carmel', found in 1 Kings 18.

Let's just set the scene again to get some context. Elijah was operating under God's orders during the reign of a king called Ahab. Ahab was a rotten egg, and continued to rule over Israel in the same way his predecessors had done (poor effort). The Bible tells us that not only was he a terrible and evil king, he was married to a woman called Jezebel (whose name quite literally means 'wicked'), who was big into worshipping false gods like Baal and Asherah. They had a following, too; the Bible says there were 450 prophets of Baal and 400 prophets of Asherah, who were all in Jezebel's camp. If that wasn't bad enough, they were also into child sacrifice. King Ahab and Queen Jezebel set about building a temple to their gods in Samaria, and the Bible tells us that not a single king before him had done so much to anger God as King Ahab had. Elijah had had enough, and he called Jezebel (and all those who sat around her table) to sort things out in a final showdown on Mount Carmel. What happens next would make a Hollywood blockbuster.

It was Elijah versus the 850 prophets of Baal, both parties trying to prove that theirs was the true God of Israel. They set up two altars (one each), both with a bull sacrifice on top. Then they called on either Baal or Yahweh (God) to zap the bulls with heavenly fire. Elijah was so confident that he drenched his entire altar with water – having dug a trench around it – just to make it even more difficult.

The hours ticked by, and as the 850 prophets of Baal danced around their altar, delirious and exhausted, nothing happened. In the middle of their frenzy of emotion and ritual, Elijah stepped up and simply prayed this:

'O LORD, God of Abraham, Isaac, and Jacob, prove today that you are God in Israel and that I am your servant. Prove that I have done all this at your command. O LORD, answer me! Answer me so these people will know that you, O LORD, are God and that you have brought them back to yourself.' (1 Kings 18:36–37)

Boom – fire from heaven tore down from above, consuming the wood, the animal, the stone, the dust and even the water. Team Baal were all somewhat stunned (and, needless to say, exhausted and in a lot of trouble). Elijah had them restrained and put to death. Brutal!

OK, there's a reason we've just gone over that. Elijah was on a high – he'd just seen a phenomenal miracle, and God had established His authority in Israel. Then this happened:

'When Ahab got home, he told Jezebel everything Elijah had done, including the way he had killed all the prophets of Baal. So Jezebel sent this message to Elijah: "May the gods strike me and even kill me if by this time tomorrow I have not killed you just as you killed them."' (1 Kings 19:1–2)

The threat, the whisper, the lie, the challenge; whatever it was to Elijah, it undid him. The Bible says he ran for his life, sat under a tree, and wished he was dead. Mount Carmel already a fading memory, Elijah ended up in a cave for the night, hiding.

Like loads of us men, Elijah had found his cave of despair and disappointment. Whatever reasons lead us to these caves, what matters is that we realise, quickly, that this is where we are. The cave of despair is a terrible place to be; it is where we are alone, isolated, frustrated, disappointed, and struggling to find any real perspective in life. But I believe it is also the place where God meets with men to awaken them – where He prods the sleeping lion and deals with us – and this is where we go against the grain. The grain is to stay in the cave, ignore it, sulk and wallow in self-pity. The grain keeps us locked in the cave until our eyes adjust and our reality doesn't seem so dark and weird anymore. Danger zone! If that's you, comfort in the cave has become your new normal.

Now you can stay in the cave and wrestle with the darkness; you can buy a self-help book and slowly crawl towards the light. Or, there is another way: surrender. The 'surrender' that Christian men are called to in these moments says, 'God, this is rubbish. I'm in a total mess and I need help. Please help me. I've run out of strength with this.'

Elijah's moment of surrender came after a moment of revelation (read the full version in 1 Kings 19). A 'revelation' is on God's terms, and is His way of letting you see more of Him. That's all. This is exactly what Elijah received, and I think this is essential for Christian men to seek when they arrive in 'the cave'. The process can be brutal, challenging and humbling – it breaks your pride, your fierce sense of independence, and your *I will dig myself out of this with my tongue if I have to* mentality. It really does go against the grain, and for Elijah, it was just the beginning of breakthrough.

David

'Purify me from my sins, and I will be clean; wash me, and I will be whiter than snow. Oh, give me back my joy again; you have broken me—now let me rejoice. Don't keep looking at my sins. Remove the stain of my guilt. Create in me a clean heart, O God. Renew a loyal spirit within me. Do not banish me from your presence, and don't take your Holy Spirit from me.' (Psalm 51:7-11)

Read about David's life in the books of 1 Samuel and 2 Samuel, and the Psalms.

The life of David, as recorded in the Bible, is a lot more than we can reflect on in this short chapter – but if we are talking about men in the Bible who went against the grain, then I really want to talk about King David. If you get the chance, take some time to look at the whole of David's story – he was able to fuse together many fascinating characteristics and attributes into one life.

To quickly set the scene: Israel had been ruled by judges, but they wanted a king, like the other nations around them. So a prophet, called Samuel, anointed (blessed into power) a king for them who God had picked out. His name was Saul, and he did OK for a while – but sadly he turned for the worse, and in the end he lost his throne (and his life) in battle. However, the transition of power following the reign of Saul was far from smooth, and this is the area I want to zoom in on for this chapter.

I described in part one how church was a huge part of my youth, and how my brother and I regularly attended various clubs, camps and activities. It was in that kind of setting that I learnt about what a Christian man should look like: honest, caring, devoted, humble, compassionate, gentle, kind and loving. This is what we were taught, and if your experience of church has been similar to mine, you might agree. We are taught that Christian men are to behave in certain ways, and our lives should reflect these values and Christlike attributes. All really good things, but this isn't the full picture; it is only half the man, but I hadn't ever noticed it. As I got older, I started to feel increasingly restless; a sort of rebellion and an unsettled feeling in me that, while I was trying to have all these qualities, I felt somewhat numb and blunted: without edge, rawness and, well, me.

Here's what I think happens. We train, teach and nurture 'safe' because we'd rather leave out the risky bits; the difficult to comprehend bits; the stuff that's a little bit too ugly to talk about at church on a Sunday. Things like raw passion – the Bible talks about it. What about indignation, and the feeling of anger that is justified and right to express? A target, a goal, a prize, a battle to be won, a high cost and a high calling, an invitation to follow Jesus and die to ourselves? What we do is train and nurture the pastor heart, the shepherd who lays down his life for the sheep. But what about the warrior, skilled in battle and ready for combat? How is he being trained and sharpened for the fight? Well, he isn't really... at least, I wasn't.

But David somehow got the balance right. He managed to fuse strength with surrender, power with worship, authority with submission. David was a skilled and able fighter, but also a songwriter and worship leader. He led a band of elite fighting men into war, but he also wrote some of the most intimate, gentle and gracious psalms in the Bible. I'm not trying to define one type of masculinity here, but what I am saying is that we can be more than just safe, gentle, meek, mild men. Talk to a soldier who also follows Jesus as his King – he will understand the call to be like Christ, the shepherd heart fused with the warrior heart. I think thousands of men are switched off from following Jesus because all they see is the invitation to be a shepherd, with no hint of adventure, risk or challenge. If that's you, let me tell you it isn't that way at all.

The last thing I want to talk about is David's surrender.

If we zoom back in on the story I started with (at the dodgy end of Saul's reign), David was being chased by Saul, who wanted to kill him. Here we have David and his men hiding in a cave (theme!). Saul popped into the cave to go to the loo (it's right there in 1 Samuel 24!), giving David and his men – who were hidden in that very same cave – the perfect chance to murder Saul, right there with his pants down, and end it all. David's men urged him to slay the king, so David crept up to him, knife in hand. But all David did was cut off a section of Saul's robe, and then he slipped away silently. As an oblivious Saul exits the cave and mounts his horse, David appears and lies before him in surrender! He puts his life into the king's hands, and refuses to kill him or attack him. David's life was full of these encounters, and moments where he simply refused to do what people around him urged him to do. He operated his life in a different way.

Have you been wronged by someone, and revenge seems justified? Do you find comfort in retaliating and hurting people who have hurt you? Have you been ripped off, had money stolen, or a bad deal that's left you with nothing, and you dream about the day of your return and their demise? The wild thing here is that Christian men are called to go *against* this grain. To surrender; to choose to bless and not curse; to yield and show forgiveness.

I honestly believe that if we can live our lives like this it will be transformational to us and others around us. Does that sound like a faith that is a crutch, an easy gig without something to fight for? No, not at all. This is so costly, men – that's part of the call to follow Jesus.

Jesus

'Jesus replied, "I tell you the truth, everyone who sins is a slave of sin. A slave is not a permanent member of the family, but a son is part of the family forever. So if the Son sets you free, you are truly free.' (John 8:34-36)

Read all about the life and miracles of Jesus in the Gospels of Matthew, Mark, Luke and John.

There is a verse in the Bible that troubles me a little bit, and it's this one:

> *'Imitate God, therefore, in everything you do, because you are his dear children. Live a life filled with love, following the example of Christ. He loved us and offered himself as a sacrifice for us, a pleasing aroma to God.' (Ephesians 5:1–2)*

I've been trying to show you that following Jesus isn't an easy thing. It involves all our energy, heart and drive. Following Jesus will take us into deep waters and uncharted seas.

My hope has been that, if you don't follow Jesus, by reading this book you will have had a glimpse of this and seen the call on your life, a huge call, to step up and make Jesus your King. My hope has also been that, if you are a Christian man, some of this has awoken and prodded that sleeping lion again. But the bar must be moved higher guys, and it happens here in this Bible verse. You see, we are called to follow Jesus, but the following is just the first phase. We are also asked to imitate Him: to be like Him, not just follow Him. Game changer.

Let me give you a brief (and by no means exhaustive) list of how Jesus went against the grain in His life.

Jesus reached out and touched the untouchable in society. He spent time with those pressed against the rough side of humanity and He loved them deeply. He didn't seek the richest places, the best seat and the best food. He walked with the down-and-outs and noticed their poverty and misery, and He helped them physically, practically, emotionally and spiritually.

Jesus used His voice and power to break down social boundaries and stigmas. He spoke with, empowered and had close friendships with women – something counter-cultural and shocking at the time. He healed a woman who had been suffering with menstrual bleeding for years – an illness that had isolated her from her community in the most painful way. She was healed, restored and brought back in. (Jesus also received support, care and provision from women as they followed Him and listened to His teaching.)

Jesus ate with (and held the friendship of) the notorious sinners and wrongdoers of the time. Tax collectors – considered to be evil men who loved to bribe and cheat – all ate around the same table as Jesus (which, in that culture, was a significant gesture of acceptance).

Jesus didn't seek promotion, power, status or a public profile that everyone would praise. He served and stayed on the fringe whenever possible. He nurtured a private life – away from the crowds, He often withdrew from others to be alone and pray.

In serving, Jesus washed feet – a tradition and custom held by slaves and house workers to welcome guests to a home. Instead of waiting to be served while sitting on a throne of supremacy and entitlement, He washed the feet of His friends. (Some of these things might have lost some of their cultural impact in today's society, but Jesus choosing to wash the feet of others was huge.)

Jesus became angry when He found corrupt traders ripping people off in the Temple. He trashed the place with a whip and kicked over all their merchandise. He didn't tether His emotion or hide behind a mask: He cried, He got angry, He shouted, He was blunt and He challenged people – all without disguise.

Jesus also didn't play into the expectations of others. He understood who He was and, more importantly, *why* He was. The Jewish people expected a rich and powerful warrior-king, yet Jesus chose no possessions, and chose to ride a donkey rather than a majestic stallion.

But for me, the most incredible example of Jesus going against the grain takes place in the Garden of Gethsemane, where He was praying on the night of His arrest. Men were about to come to take Him, falsely accuse Him, beat Him, whip and flog Him, dress Him as a mock 'king' and nail Him to a cross. And there in the garden, at Jesus' greatest hour of need, His friends were *asleep*. Yet He didn't accuse them – He just let them sleep. As Jesus was arrested, He didn't fight back, He didn't protest and call for a lawyer; He just accepted it. Even when Peter freaked out and cut the ear off one of the soldiers, Jesus responded by healing the man's ear, refusing even then to have a go.

Jesus was lied about to His face, but didn't defend Himself. He was beaten and spat on, but didn't fight back. He was nailed to a wooden cross, and after hanging there for hours, He called out, 'It is finished.' And those words, spoken as Jesus died, have to be the ultimate act of going against the grain: love overcame hate, life overcame death, mercy and grace won. And because of this moment, you, me and anyone who calls on the name of Jesus will be saved.

You might be thinking, *Mate, I'm not about to let someone stick me on a cross, I can't be like Jesus like that!* True, but Jesus invites you to carry your own 'cross' – to be like Him in surrendering your life, your control and your power to Him. In reality, this is about dying – dying to ourselves, and letting Him take control.

This is where the rubber hits the road, and where the real cost to following Jesus starts to kick in. The invitation Jesus extends isn't for you to play nice on a Sunday, look the part and put your 'eternal life entry ticket' under your pillow until you die. The call Jesus puts to men like me and you is to follow Him all the way, to be ready to face ridicule, persecution, rejection and difficulty. Our call is to be ready to follow His lead and to forgive, show kindness, generosity, patience and self-control. We're not called to be men who are pushed around, rudderless through life, but men with conviction and grit; men with purpose, vision and marching orders. This isn't some legalistic set of nice ideas to make life easy and amenable; this road can and might lead you to what the world might label as failure, but that isn't the way Jesus measures success.

I have seen men walk away from £70k bonuses to follow a conviction to step out in their faith in Jesus. New cars, houses, holidays, security – this has all been pushed aside to make way for something deeper that Jesus has called them to follow. Men have silently given hundreds of thousands of pounds so that other men might hear the truth about Jesus. They didn't give this money with a great announcement, but privately and with no chance of a pat on the back.

These men might not even see the results of these decisions in their lifetime – they may be laying foundations for the next generation to reap the harvest – but these men operate against the world's logic and reason. They refuse to conform, and instead adventurously look for trouble, creativity and paths to stretch their faith. They welcome difficulty; they face-palm the armies of doubters and armchair critics watching from the sidelines. This is their moment to run, to excel and to follow Jesus who has transformed their lives and efforts for even greater things. These men don't look for recognition from the world, they run from it. Their energy comes from another place – another person – and they refuse to be stopped.

Peter

'At this point many of his disciples turned away and deserted him. Then Jesus turned to the Twelve and asked, "Are you also going to leave?" Simon Peter replied, "Lord, to whom would we go? You have the words that give eternal life. We believe, and we know you are the Holy One of God."' (John 6:66-69)

Read about Peter in the Gospels, and the books of 1 Peter and 2 Peter (letters he wrote).

If there's one man in the Bible who really brings this stuff home for men like us, it's Peter. Peter was one of Jesus' disciples – one of His closest friends who followed Him and journeyed with Him.

Peter wasn't exactly the religious elite. He wasn't even particularly educated, except from the school of life. A fisherman by trade, he was a grafter – but often went with his heart and not his head. He was a man of action, but also a man who knew what it was like to get stuff wrong and have to pick himself back up again. Peter was impulsive, and if he saw an opportunity or an open door, he would take it. He stayed well clear of the ruts that so many of us fellas get stuck in, and refused to be put into a box that defined him for the rest of his life.

It's pretty awesome how Jesus first called Peter to follow Him. Peter had just come back in after a pretty disappointing night of fishing, when Jesus piped up with a bit of advice: 'go out where it is deeper' (Luke 5:4). Probably a bit miffed, Peter did it – and the catch of fish was *massive*. Totally in awe of this bloke in his boat, Peter had to face up to his own sin and the stark contrast of the life he had been living. He says to Jesus, 'Oh, Lord, please leave me—I'm such a sinful man.' Peter knew in his heart he wasn't perfect, and he had baggage, just like me and you. Jesus invited Peter to follow Him – to just leave the boat and the nets there and then – to quit the day job and follow Him. The Bible tells us that's exactly what Peter did. He must have felt unworthy; he must have felt like getting as far away as he could from this holy man who showed up the mess in his own life just by being near, but he followed Jesus nonetheless.

During his three-year journey with Jesus, Peter had no shortage of misunderstandings – and I can totally relate to that! On one occasion, when Jesus was talking about His death, Peter actually stepped in to *correct* Jesus. And Jesus was having none of it! He turned to Peter, saying, 'Get away from me, Satan!' If Jesus had said that to me I would have died of embarrassment, or at least left the group, never to be seen again (especially after being called Satan!). But not Peter: mistakes, failure and saying the wrong thing were all part of the journey. Let's look at a couple more...

When Jesus was arrested in the Garden of Gethsemane (as we saw in the previous chapter), it was Peter who pulled out a concealed blade and sliced the ear clean off a soldier. But instead of a reassuring nod of 'Cheers, Pete!' from Jesus, he got rebuked again. Jesus even put the bloke's ear back on in front of everyone (awkward). Peter got it wrong – again.

As Jesus was led away to trial and the false witnesses turned up, Peter was recognised (and accused) three times as being part of the Jesus gang. Scared for his own skin, Peter rejected the accusations, insisting that he had never met Him in his life – just as Jesus had said he would. *Ouch*. Almost immediately, Peter had a defining moment in tears, realising he'd just given Judas a run for his money in the betrayal department.

You might think that after feeling like a rotten sinner, saying and doing the wrong things around Jesus on more than one occasion, Peter would shrink away into obscurity – but no chance! Peter became one of the central driving forces of the Early Church, and as he died on a cross upside down, being murdered for loving Jesus, he was victorious.

Peter didn't live his life under the label 'failure'. Peter's the guy who walked on water when everyone else was too afraid (or in shock) to step out of the boat. Do you know this story? A storm was rising (slight understatement – the boat was tipping enough to make even seasoned fishermen look like seasick tourists). As the storm thrashed the boat, the men saw what looked like a ghost walking on the water – and they soon recognised it to be Jesus! Against all rationale, Peter called out to Jesus something along the lines of, 'If that's You, invite me out onto the water with You!' Jesus did, and out he got. He literally stepped out of the boat, onto the sea, and walked towards Jesus. In the middle of a storm. I'm not sure what else to say here, but just imagine for a moment – shut your eyes and picture yourself taking steps on the sea. Wow.

All the natural laws that our minds are locked into are, in that moment, undone. Jesus has all authority, even over the sea; how Peter's body stayed within that natural order, no one knows. But Peter walked on water, and as he himself came to terms with what was happening, the laws of physics rushed back into his mind: *Surely, this is impossible.* And here's what's really interesting – it's only when he took his eyes off Jesus that he began to sink. (Immediately, Jesus pulled him up and they both got back onto the boat, but what a moment!)

Here is the thing: for me, being a Christian man is about being willing to look at Jesus in ways that will defy our reason, logic and rationale. If you're not a Christian, then the challenge is to see this Jesus not as just a 'good man' or 'good teacher'; He invites you to see Him as the Son of God, nothing else. Surely this goes against the grain of everything the world would tell us. How can this be? God's *Son*? This is the great and beautiful mystery of the Bible, but it requires a lot of faith, and the willingness to refuse what you think you know.

If you are a Christian, then I want to invite you to go against the grain of your existing paradigms and re-imagine the scale on which Jesus can work: the lives you think are beyond rescue; the situations you think are beyond healing and rebuilding; your kids and the decisions they make that confuse you and leave you desperate for God to do something. Or maybe you have been wearing some of Peter's labels, and feel like these are never going to fade. Refuse them. Even when we fail, we can stand again. Peter discovered this resurrection DNA in following Jesus; down and out just isn't an option.

Paul

'And I am convinced that nothing
can ever separate us from God's love.
Neither death nor life, neither angels
nor demons, neither our fears for today
nor our worries about tomorrow—not
even the powers of hell can separate
us from God's love. No power in the
sky above or in the earth below—
indeed, nothing in all creation will ever
be able to separate us from the love of
God that is revealed in Christ Jesus our
Lord.' (Romans 8:38-39)

*Read about Paul in loads of the New Testament in the Bible!
(The book of Acts is a good place to start...)*

The men in the Bible who went against the grain discovered
the freedom in God that enabled them to move past their
mistakes, guilt and shame. And Paul in particular had
significant cause for guilt and shame – but still managed
to move forward in his life and relationship with God in

incredible ways. Seriously – this guy wrote huge chunks of the New Testament.

But Paul had a dodgy past, to say the least. He was originally known as Saul, and had set himself up as the most active hater of Christians and the Early Church. He hadn't met Jesus (this was a few years after His return to heaven), but he worked very hard to systematically round up Christians and see them imprisoned. In one such case, a young man called Stephen was on trial for his faith in Jesus, when the mob decided to stone him to death. There in the crowd, holding the coats of the men throwing the stones was Saul – no doubt delighted at the whole event.

Saul went on to have a serious encounter with Jesus while on his way to a popular Christian area for a spot of rounding up and persecuting. Blinded by a piercing heavenly light, and transformed by a conversation with the audible voice of Jesus, Saul emerged as Paul, about to embark on a radical life change. He gave up his persecution of Christians, instead become the driving force for the Early Church's growth across much of the world. (Read the full story in Acts 9.)

Reading about Paul always leaves me with a question. How can you go from being a bloke who systematically causes untold pain and misery, a man who actively despises God, to being a man who knows he is forgiven, and spends the rest of his life telling others about Jesus? The good news is the same power that transformed Paul is at work for you and me today. It's called 'grace'. The grace that God invites us to receive is about us becoming new men, 'born again' by the Holy Spirit of God and equipped and tasked to a new way of living. We get to start all over again with a spiritual re-birth, brand new and forgiven. The Bible is full of men and women who have found this grace. It's not something we can earn or work for or deserve; it's not given because of our merits and achievements, but by what Jesus accomplished on the cross.

But the bit that actually goes against the grain is Paul's ability to accept this 'grace invitation'. All around the UK, I've seen so many blokes so locked into the failures of their past that they struggle to move forward. I think it's strange, but so many people want to do something before they feel God will be ready to forgive them or welcome them home. I remember speaking at a church in Middlesbrough with a good mate of mine called Swanny, and he explained it like this: 'It's like trying to get well before going to the doctor. It just doesn't make sense.' The reason grace is so amazing is that it grabs hold of you where you are now and lets you move on, forgiven and free, all because Jesus gave everything for you on the cross.

Does this mean no consequences then? No, not at all – if you kill someone, and then accept the grace and forgiveness of God, you still live under the law of the land and its justice system (and that person is still dead). But if we are willing to accept grace, we don't have to stay enslaved to that guilt and shame. This involves going against the grain of our instincts, our ideas about justice and what we think we deserve, and often, our pride. But we need to say yes to Jesus, and let the gift of grace do its work in our lives.

After accepting the amazing gift of grace, Paul went on to write lots of letters to churches and individuals (which now make up quite a lot of the New Testament); he planted churches, became a roaming evangelist, and saw the most amazing miracles happen. But there is one more thing I want to take from the life of Paul that goes against the grain perhaps more than anything else: suffering. Paul's journeys (on his way to tell people about Jesus) didn't always go well. He was shipwrecked, beaten up, chased out of towns and communities, imprisoned, flogged, left for dead on a few occasions, and bitten by a snake. In the end, Paul was beheaded after being held prisoner for years – but somehow, despite all this adversity and chaos, he kept moving forwards. He didn't allow anything to slow him down. If anything, it fuelled him to fight harder.

When chaos hits my life, I retreat. I hide and spend time feeling sorry for myself, playing the world's largest violin to a tune called self-pity (it has lots of verses, too). But when Paul was in prison after being severely beaten for his faith, he refused to get dragged down into despair. He took all of that pain and turned it into praise (literally singing in the cell and leading all the other prisoners to do the same!). It's just incredible. I don't think anyone can look at this and justifiably say that the Christian faith is for wimps. To turn the trials and troubles in our lives into fuel for worship goes against the grain in a way that might give us splinters, but will show just how much God can do in our lives.

The call on Christian men to live out genuine faith like this is phenomenal. Acknowledging pain and trouble, and through tears and honesty letting them be part of your story, is counter-instinctive. So is turning *to* God, not away from Him. That is going against the grain, and for me, raises the bar yet again on what following Jesus is all about.

The disciples

"'[These men] have caused trouble all over the world," they shouted, "and now they are here disturbing our city, too... They are all guilty of treason against Caesar, for they profess allegiance to another king, named Jesus.'" (Acts 17:6-7)

Read about the journey, acts and legacies of the disciples throughout the New Testament.

I want to finish this section with a quick look at the disciples – a simple bunch of fellas who spent time with Jesus, watched Him, trusted Him and lived to follow Him and be like Him. These men were not perfect – many of them were plucked from the bottom of society's list of next big shakers – but they made Jesus' list. These men went out into the world, faced terrifying situations, were thrown in prison and suffered at the hands of merciless people. Killed, martyred, exiled and humiliated for their trust in Jesus, these men (with the exception of John) boldly walked to early deaths without turning their backs on the Jesus who had set them free.

What's so remarkable about this is that these disciples – these friends of Jesus – didn't turn the world upside down with war, weapons and power. They didn't use force and manipulation, or turn to bribes and underhand dealing to gain a foothold. They operated with grace, mercy, kindness, gentleness, compassion, forgiveness, truth and love. That didn't make them pushovers and softies. It made them slice through bitterness, hostility and anger; it made them pierce the hearts of the powerful; it gave them the keys to nations and civilisations. This band of misfits became troublemakers with Jesus' truth, presence and power – and that, men, is the greatest invitation ever.

Are you in? Are you willing to go against the grain and live beyond the sofas of conformity? Are you willing to refuse the world's expectations and let Jesus guide your life, your actions and your heart? Are you willing to be more like Jesus, to follow Him and let that journey shape you into a new man? Are you tired of *hearing* about what God is doing, and want to *see* Him do it and be part of it? Are you tired of your disbelief and your logic-processor washing all this stuff away?

To follow Jesus and seek to be like Him in how you act, react and live your life will be the greatest adventure and journey you ever embark on. He won't leave you to it, either – He promises to be with you, even until the very end. It won't get much better than that, so if you want to find yourself, go

against the grain and then lose yourself, an incredible life
awaits you behind the door – if you dare.

Part 3

Action stations

So, that's all great – but how do we do it?

Perhaps you have read this and you are totally up for it – you have decided to follow Jesus and you are all-in, 100%. Or maybe you made a decision to follow Jesus earlier on in your life, but somewhere along the journey the whole thing slowed down to a crawl, then barely anything at all, and you've been looking for the closest set of defibrillating paddles to kick-start your heart again. Or maybe the defibrillating paddles have got you moving again, but now what? How do you do this stuff and go against the grain?

Let me offer some practical suggestions. Take one of these a day for the next week. Don't rush it; read it, then chew it over during the day, see if it fits and has an impact on your life. Then, at the end of the week, do something about it! Call, invite, speak… whatever, just do it.

(Just to mention, you might take a month going over this stuff. I spent a month praying the same thing every morning, looking for the fire! I'm not suggesting this is just seven days and then move on. Take your time.)

Day 1: Fire

No amount of reading Christian books and listening to church sermons will put the kind of lasting fire in your heart that I've been talking about. There is a part here that we need to discover – it is the work of the Holy Spirit in our lives. Sure, listening to talks and reading a good book (like this one!) will stir the brain and heart for a time, but they won't light a lasting fire.

Jeremiah, a prophet in the Old Testament, said something interesting about the sort of fire I am banging on about, and it is this:

'But if I say I'll never mention the LORD or speak in his name, his word burns in my heart like a fire. It's like a fire in my bones! I am worn out trying to hold it in! I can't do it!' (Jeremiah 20:9)

This fire is essential, men, and it comes from asking God to put it in your heart. I have seen guys who have been going to church for more than 20 years accept Jesus for the first time, and break out of years of just going to church and just playing the part of a follower of Jesus; men who realised that on the outside they could be seen to be Christians, but they had no fire in their hearts.

The fire is about a deep desire, even yearning, which moves us in a profound way to not want to watch our life ebb away without being involved in what I call heaven's agenda. This deep stirring in our hearts is about a message of hope that we love; a Captain and Master who we serve to the very end; it is about a man who gave everything to set us free.

Need that fire? Then ask for it – I really do think it's that simple.

There have been moments in my life when I've known the need for this fire, and the secret to getting it is to ask God for it in prayer. Perhaps, like me, you'll know the feeling of, 'Ohhhh, *prayer*!' It's never been something I've done particularly well, to be honest, but I can tell you that when I have gone after God in prayer and made it a discipline, and I've asked Him to meet me and bring the fire, it has happened.

Find guys to pray with, set time aside and build it in as a routine. It won't be easy, but relationships can really help us with our prayer lives. And that leads me on to the practical idea for day two…

Day 2: Relationship

If you are seeking to go against the grain as a follower of Jesus, I would definitely encourage you to find some good mates, and lean on them.

Having seen loads of men's groups meeting together as part of my role at CVM, I have seen the incredible impact of this in men's lives. Guys who have been lost in society, addicted to drugs, drink, porn and gambling have found answers, help and new life through the simple thing of men meeting together. I have seen men with hidden pasts vomit them out and find freedom; men sharing insecurity, weakness, failure and shame. I have seen men of influence, power and notability in society find strength and courage, accountability and lifelines in these gatherings.

When we align ourselves with this stuff, we allow a process of relationship that can be healing, inspirational and deeply moving for us. Taking this a step further, once trust has been built and we feel we can turn up with an undefended heart, we can find that things in our lives begin to be dealt with.

Find a band of brothers who will call stuff out in your life, keep you focused, sharp and on task. Find the men who will remember to ask you how that massive meeting went, or what happened in that difficult conversation you had recently. This stuff matters.

Day 3: Story

Building on this framework of relationship with other fellas, knowing and owning your story – and hearing the stories of others – is essential when going against the grain.

Jesus used parables for good reason. A story evokes a response, and invites you to imagine and picture yourself within it – what would you do, say, or think? Having space to tell your story, where other men will listen and not interrupt, talk over or try to fix your life and experience, is incredibly empowering. Your story isn't just the last 30, 40 or however many years back you go; it is tomorrow, the week after next, and so on. Your story is continually unfolding, and having a way in which it can be shared (and therefore be an encouragement to others) is important on this journey.

When we tell of our encounters, battles, scars, wounds, moments of fear and moments of courage, we start to unlock something unique. If it works (and it might not for all men – the location is down to you), I would encourage doing this around a fire.

And that leads me on to the next bit.

Day 4: Vulnerability in action

If I'm expected to be open and honest – to share the deep caverns in my life – it won't happen if you stuff me into a 20-minute time slot of 'being vulnerable'. If, however, you sit me around a fire – and as we burn stuff, the heat of the fire on my face and the cold of the night on my back make me feel connected to the fire in some way, and therefore to the men around me in some way – I will share from a place of vulnerability, and be open to grow from the experience.

I have found this to be true in other ways too: watching a football match, having a pint, walking a hill, fixing a fence, carrying a sofa to the tip together... You get the picture – it's an opportunity to share deeply in the kind of environments that will be effective. Be creative; find the places you enjoy being in and invite the fellas along. Do life in a real way, and if you want to go against the grain in your journey following Jesus, these times will be a valuable acquisition you won't easily give up.

Day 5: Affirmation

We touched on this nerve already when we looked at the story of the prodigal son, but I want to mention it again here because this one really makes a difference. Think of it this way: where do you get your affirmation from?

'Well done, mate, nice job on that brickwork today.'

'Nice one in the meeting today, you nailed it in there.'

'Dad, you're the best dad ever! Happy Father's Day.'

'To the husband I love, Happy Valentine's Day.'

As men, we crave affirmation; we long to hear things that will affirm who we are and how well we have done. I know that as soon as we start to consider what it means to be 'good enough', there might be an immediate connection to sex – so let's just call that one out straight away. There is so much more to this stuff than whether or not we perform sexually and get the affirmation we strive for.

Am I 'good enough'? Am I a good enough husband, father, employee, son, brother, boss, uncle, friend, role model or leader? I have heard so many stories from men who sought affirmation in their lives and struggled to find it; they wanted it from positive sources initially, but when that couldn't be found, affirmation in negative forms would do.

The hunger and desperation for affirmation; the unfulfilled searching that leaves us feeling lost and fragile – this all gets buried beneath the stiff-upper-lip code of manliness, never to be visited again, ever!

I have struggled to give affirmation and wrestled even more to receive it, but it is essential for us to go after this stuff. In building on this relationship framework with story, and vulnerability in action, we can find positive and healthy affirmation (and give it too). It might feel like someone is running their nails down a blackboard the first few times you hear something positive spoken over you, but go with it – let it in! It works.

Day 6: Random acts of kindness

Let me share with you something I am discovering: opportunities are just opportunities to *act*. An opportunity is meaningless until you actually *do* something!

As I have invested in these intentional relationships that help me go against the grain, I've seen the importance of encouraging each other to do random acts of kindness. Remember what I suggested before about getting in tune with the Holy Spirit and watching for the small, random prompts that come up? These prompts will only ever be a mere opportunity, a moment that will pass and fade, unless we make something of that moment.

I was on a train recently, having bagged a cheap first-class seat, and I was one hour into my two-hour trip home. First class was over-booked, and people were getting angry and heated about the seat they'd paid for and couldn't have (quite understandably!). Sitting in my lovely, comfy seat, I felt a 'spiritual' nudge, and it went like this: 'Nathan, offer your seat to one of these people. Explain that you have had it for an hour, and for the last hour of your journey, you want to share it with someone who has paid for a first-class seat too. Just offer it, and stand for the last hour of the trip.'

What I want to suggest is that, in being part of these honest relationships with a group of men, we invite the process of positive random acts to be encouraged, inspired, and carried out. We can do this stuff, take the opportunities, and share with the guys what happens when we stick our necks out to be generous, brave, risky etc. So… what happened on the train?

Truth is, I looked out of the window, completed level 291 on Candy Crush on my phone, and completely ignored the opportunity. I am being honest here! Remember, it is only an opportunity until you do something with it. Don't ignore it – go and see what happens.

Day 7: Stay sharp

Just like Admiral Ackbar during the battle of Endor in *Star Wars: Return of the Jedi*, let me start by saying, 'It's a trap!'

If you want to go against the grain – and have heard what I've said about relationship, story, vulnerability, honesty and affirmation – then you need to be aware that there's a trap. Some of these groups of men that gather can, inadvertently, end up living out all that I've covered in part one by going *with* the grain, and never against it. We can fall into the trap of simply being superficial, never really breaking the malaise or diving head-first into the reality of what life is like – the big questions, the horrible stuff we carry, and the wins we secretly aim for. The challenge here is to not give up, or believe that the group won't ever change or be shaped differently. Work at change from the inside out: show up and be the guy who is in this for the long haul, always learning and being willing to get behind the group.

This isn't easy, because if it doesn't instantly work for us, we vote with our feet and walk. But try to stay with it. I am speaking to myself here, but I believe we can see great progress if we keep the against-the-grain DNA in our hearts. It is real, gritty, raw and honest, and men will respond to it.

This DNA takes us right back to day one of this section. You keep the fire alive and let it shape the DNA of multiplication and evangelism, and task the group to be on a rescue mission to reach more men. It is essential that we fight to keep that fire alive; be tooled up to share Jesus; be focused on letting our lives be made like Him, in His image, and see men's lives transformed by Him.

But it can be easy for groups to lose this fire; they meet, eat, rinse, repeat. There is no rawness, vulnerability or mining of their lives. They open the Bible, faithfully explore passages and try to apply them to the next day they go into, but there needs to be more. Imagine what it might look like if you threw some of these suggestions out there:

- How will this truth hit your life this week?
- What are you praying about this week?
- Who are you praying for this week?
- Let's hear from you again next week to see how it went!
- What can we do this year to share Jesus together, as well as on our own?
- Can we go and do something in the community in the next few months?
- Let's all put £40 in a pot and pray for wisdom to see where we can give it, and see what God does.
- Let's hear from Colin/Dave/Steve or whoever tonight as they have stuff to share and lay down.
- Fellas, I need to confess some stuff. This week I went back to this... I started looking at this again... I have

been having these thoughts again... Please pray for me; hold me accountable and help me to beat this stuff.

- Guys, my wife and I are in desperate need...
- Men, I need help... I am gambling secretly, I am looking at loads of porn, I am thinking about ending my life... help me, men.
- I am struggling with disbelief, guys. I am feeling so inadequate and not enough. I am out of my depth at work... help me.
- I am angry again. I feel it bubbling up all the time.
- I am feeling bitter about life and my sexual relationship with my wife.
- I am lonely, guys, and need a life partner.

Does any of this ring true? Can you see the radical and polar opposites of a group of men gathering and reading a Bible verse and a commentary and then going home, to a drastically real and full-on commitment to one another?

My hope is that as you fight for this stuff, you will find incredible victory in your own life and the lives around you. I am convinced that Jesus can and does work in varied and limitless ways; He is bigger than any ideas I could ever have. But I do believe we are tasked with a great challenge and a life call to make disciples – to see men meet Jesus in a real way – and I believe this will happen when we go against the grain together.

More good reads for men

52 MEN OF THE BIBLE
Dig deeper into the lives of some of the men in the Bible. From Adam to Jesus, explore how their example can affect your walk with God.
Author: Carl Beech
ISBN: 978-1-78259-154-2

MAN PRAYER MANUAL
Consider real-life stories of prayer and breakthrough, and be encouraged to live a dynamic life of prayer.
Author: Carl Beech
ISBN: 978-1-78259-522-9

IRON MEN
Just as iron sharpens iron, Nathan looks at how Christian men can help sharpen each other in their faith.
Author: Nathan Blackaby
ISBN: 978-1-78259-672-1

Also available in eBook format

CWR in partnership with ᑕᐯM
For the full range of products, current prices and to order visit
www.cwr.org.uk/shop
Also available from Christian bookshops.

Explore key aspects of the Christian faith

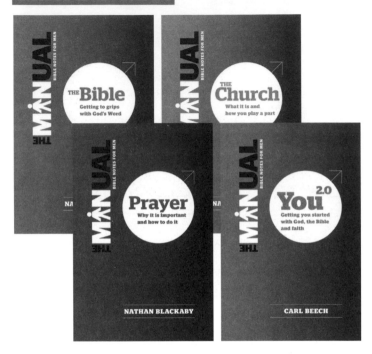

Packed with 30 relevant Bible readings, practical points and prayers, these notes will help you understand the foundations of Christianity and build your relationship with God.

Also available in eBook format

For the full range of products, current prices and to order visit
www.cwr.org.uk/shop
Also available from Christian bookshops.

Daily Bible reading notes for men by Carl Beech

These undated Bible notes explore different themes to encourage and challenge. Written by Carl Beech and two guest contributors, each book contains two months of daily readings and prayers.

Also available in eBook format

For the full range of products, current prices and to order visit **www.cwr.org.uk/shop** Also available from Christian bookshops.

Courses and seminars

Waverley Abbey College

Publishing and media

Conference facilities

Transforming lives

CWR's vision is to enable people to experience personal transformation through applying God's Word to their lives and relationships.

Our Bible-based training and resources help people around the world to:
• Grow in their walk with God
• Understand and apply Scripture to their lives
• Resource themselves and their church
• Develop pastoral care and counselling skills
• Train for leadership
• Strengthen relationships, marriage and family life and much more.

Our insightful writers provide daily Bible reading notes and other resources for all ages, and our experienced course designers and presenters have gained an international reputation for excellence and effectiveness.

CWR's Training and Conference Centre in Surrey, England, provides excellent facilities in idyllic settings – ideal for both learning and spiritual refreshment.

CWR Applying God's Word
to everyday life and relationships

CWR, Waverley Abbey House,
Waverley Lane, Farnham,
Surrey GU9 8EP, UK

Telephone: **+44 (0)1252 784700**
Email: **info@cwr.org.uk**
Website: **www.cwr.org.uk**

Registered Charity No. 294387
Company Registration No. 1990308